HOPEFUL KIDS

A revolutionary solution for empowering your kids
to create the lives they want.

LEONARD P. CASH, PH.D.

HOPEFUL
Living

ISBN 978-0-615-35567-2
Printed in Canada
10 9 8 7 6 5 4 3 2 1

www.hopefulkids.com

I dedicate this work to my source of hope, Jesus Christ, and to all those who are, and to all those who are becoming a hopeful generation.

"Hopeful Kids is terrific! It is an excellent way to empower parents and children of any age to think positive and self-motivate. The activities are easy to follow and will spark excellent conversations between adults and their kids."

Julie Aigner Clark, Founder of Baby Einstein and The Safe Side.

Contents

Foreword

Kids Need Hope! Hope gives them a belief that they can create the lives they want. Hope gives them a reason to learn new things—a reason to value one's self, others, and life itself. Hope gives them self-identity, purpose and meaning, a respect of others, and ultimately PERSONAL POWER.

Dr. Leonard Cash – Dr. Hope – brings 20 years of hands-on experience in promoting hope in mentally ill and disabled adults as well as society's toughest kids. Hopeful Kids brings you a practical, easy-to-use solution that draws upon the most effective strategies for guiding parents to help their son or daughter become a Hopeful Kid who believes, "I can create the life I want through positive choices and goals."

Through the inspiring Hopeful Kids program, developed especially for families by Dr. Cash, you will learn how to:

- Empower your kids to discover their purpose and build the lives they want
- Show your kids how to have open, no-limits communication with you so they will come to you first when faced with life-altering challenges
- Teach your kids to solve life's challenges so they are inspired to persevere in the face of adversity and overcome peer pressure and poor decision-making
- Develop your kids' confidence and competence to make positive choices and achieve life-enhancing goals

Introduction

HOPE.

You hear about it all the time. Politicians love to boast about hope. Preachers identify it as a critical element to spiritual development. Psychologists claim we need hope for our mental well-being. Professors teach that hope is the inspiration behind great works of art, science, and literature.

As a probation officer, I watched troubled youth go from being thieves, thugs, drug dealers, and gang-bangers to college graduates, clinical therapists, business owners, and even a famous chef. While working as a rehabilitation counselor and executive, I witnessed disabled men and women gain remarkable confidence and passion, then go on to achieve their dreams. I remember one man in particular who developed a whale-watching company in the Pacific Northwest. Another became a job-development counselor and helped others realize their ideal jobs; he went on to become a motivational speaker. While serving as a director of parks and recreation, I was impressed to see how former gang members, at-risk youth, and people from every imaginable socioeconomic background turned their lives around and forged a path toward a better future. And finally, as a family court administrator, I've seen families that were destined for destruction ask for and recieve help to become functional, loving families. What made the difference?

One word: HOPE!

Yes, hope is the catalyst to motivating ordinary people to accomplish extraordinary things. But what is hope? Simply defined, hope is a favorable expectation of the future. It is a belief that change is possible. Put another way, hope is a confident and optimistic outlook on life.

Those who turn their unfortunate circumstances around somehow believe they can! They believe they don't have to settle for being victims, being trapped, being at a loss as to how to build their lives. Instead, they believe they can do something that will build the lives they want. This is hope. With it, people learn to go from being victims to victors who believe they can create the lives they want through positive choices and goals. This is the definition of a hopeful person.

Hope is powerful. Better said, hope is personal power in action. This revelation led to the creation of the HOPEFUL KIDS book you now hold in your hands. We don't have to wait until the bottom falls out of our kids' lives; we can give them the power to keep that from happening and become full of hope—hopeful. This is exactly why I developed HOPEFUL KIDS to help you, parents, empower your kids to make positive choices and build purposeful lives. Through hope, we can accomplish this one kid and one family at a time.

My promise is to show you how to instill hope in your sons and daughters so that they can become hopeful kids and realize their personal power to develop the lives they want. Hope is vital to becoming masters of our own lives, developing the capacity to manage change and create meaningful lives through purposeful choices and actions. This is precisely what you will learn how to do with HOPEFUL KIDS. Moreover, as you apply these hope-inspiring principles to your family, you too will become full of hope and discover your personal power. Hope is the best way to give yourself and your kids the gift of life.

By choosing HOPEFUL KIDS, you have made one of the best investments you will ever make in your children. Ultimately, you have chosen the solution for empowering your kids to realize their God-given potential. Welcome to this awesome journey.

CHAPTER 1

The Case for Hopefulness

Our children see horrible stuff. Things children should not see. Things that make parents turn off the television and put away the newspaper when kids enter the room. Despite our best efforts, though, our kids hear about terrorism, school shootings, suicide, workplace murders, kidnapping, domestic violence, war, drugs—the list goes on. And some children actually live through the violence, rather than just seeing it on television. Don't be fooled into thinking this could never happen to your family.

LOOKING FOR HOPE

Our young people want and need hope. Hope gives them a belief that they can create the life they want. Hope gives them a reason to live—a reason to value one's self, others, and life itself. Hope gives them self-identity, purpose and meaning, a respect of others, and, ultimately—personal power. Hope can save our kids—your kids. Therefore, we must work together to help America's youth go from a hopeless generation to a hopeful generation.

The best way to give our young people a solid sense of self-respect, an appreciation of others, and a strong desire to live is to help them develop hope: a belief that they matter and are capable of creating the life they want. Hope is the process by which we can help our young people to "Get a life!"

Children need hope, plain and simple. Hope is a confident outlook on life and a belief that change is possible. This is what is missing in our shoot 'em up, throw 'em out society. America needs hope, you need hope, and, without question, your kids need hope! Hope gives us the power to create the life we want. Hope is the difference between those who live as victors or victims.

With hope comes personal power over the madness destroying America's most cherished and valuable resource—our kids. It really is a matter of life or death. No city, family, or child is immune to the deadly effects of hopelessness. In response, this book is focused on action rather than reaction, solutions rather than lip service. Our time together will disturb you, enlighten you, inspire you, but mostly it will move you to take action to save your kids. And yes, it will be hard work, but the good news is, it will be the most rewarding work you will ever undertake.

I often tell people that I have the second most important job in America: helping parents develop Hopeful Kids. You, however, as parents have the most important job: saving your kids by guiding them to become hopeful. The result? Your children will have no reason to get caught up in the forces that lead to a life of poor behavior, bad choices, and victimization. Here is why: Hopeful Kids are self-directed by an inner purpose to create the life they want. They accomplish this by making life-enhancing choices that are directed toward the achievement of positive goals. In simple words, they are fueled by personal power rather than peer pressure. Further, as a direct result of using this program with your child, you too will experience a transformation—you will become a hopeful parent.

HOPEFUL KIDS is the culmination of two decades of experience and years of research. This inspiring program was exclusively developed for the unique needs of families. It is a practical, easy-to-use, how-to solution that draws upon the most effective strategies for guiding parents to help their son or daughter become a Hopeful Kid who confidently says, "I can create the life I want through positive choices and goals." When children believe they can do this, they have become Hopeful Kids and will be well on their way to living the lives they want. Our time together will show you exactly how to accomplish this life-saving mission, step-by-step.

This program can help you to develop a Hopeful Kid regardless of your child's age. It is never too early or too late to begin cultivating hope in anyone, young or old. In general, though, this program targets school-age children, five to fifteen years old, because of their developmental levels and capacities. Nevertheless, you will find many strategies that will work for younger children. Conversely, if your kids are young adults, you will also find numerous ways to generate a greater capacity for hope. Moreover, keep in mind this program is also intended to guide you to become hopeful because Hopeful Kids come from Hopeful Parents. So in reality your child's age really doesn't matter. What matters most is that you begin using this book to discover the strategies that work best for your son or daughter.

Ideally, two parents would participate in this program with their child or children. If this is not possible, one parent or caregiver can still make a significant difference. The philosophy of this program is best summarized by saying, "It only takes the hope of one to create hope in the life of another one." If there are two, great, and if not, one is all that is required. If you have more than one child, I recommend using the HOPEFUL KIDS program with all of them together, but you can also take an individual approach. You know your kids and your situation best, so you decide what works best for your family.

Additionally, this book will serve you best if you use it: write in it, dog-ear pages, highlight inspiring passages, and constantly refer to it. Use it for personal motivation and as a support system for your action plan. In other words, do whatever it takes to make it work for your family. The HOPEFUL experience will be more enjoyable if you constantly remind yourself this is truly a journey. Don't worry about getting there immediately. Between here and there allow yourself the opportunity to live, love, laugh, and learn along the way. Assume this flexible posture and you will soon discover that with each new challenge and resulting victory, you and your child will become that much more hopeful.

CHAPTER 2

Becoming Hopeful

Hopeful people are driven by and led by purpose. Purpose underscores their decisions, interactions, beliefs, and attitudes. They are characterized by an infectious optimism, a quiet confidence, and a zest for living. To them, life is an adventure ripe with opportunity. This does not mean, however, that hopeful people are superhuman. Rather, they are just as likely as anyone to experience setbacks, pain, and suffering. The difference is how they perceive and handle life's problems. Hopeful people, by their very nature, believe they can create the life they want through their positive choices and goals. This is the true essence of being hopeful. Hopeful people are best described as ordinary people who live extraordinary lives because they possess a strong sense of personal power. They achieve this through focused, purposeful action.

DEVELOPING A HOPEFUL KID

HOPEFUL KIDS centers on helping parents develop their kids' confidence and competence to make positive choices and achieve life-enhancing goals—purpose. When kids are hopeful, they see no purpose or value in associating with negative peers or to be violent as a way to prove themselves to others. They are focused on making positive choices that result in positive outcomes. Because of their keen sense of purpose, they are much less likely to become a victim or engage in behaviors that hurt others. In other words, Hopeful Kids value themselves and others because they believe they have a greater purpose in life.

With this in mind, a Hopeful Kid is most accurately characterized by and defined by the Hopeful Motto: "I can create the life I want through positive choices and goals." The net result of this hope-filled attitude and approach to life is young people who have personal power: personal power over themselves, personal power over peer pressure, and personal power over hopelessness. Let's take a closer look at the key terms of this motto to give you a better understanding of why it is the heart of HOPEFUL:

"I can create the life I want through positive choices and goals."

I can...
Hopeful Kids believe in their ability to create the life they want through positive choices and goals. These goals constitute their purpose.

create...
Hopeful Kids have the confidence and competence to set into motion purposeful action that will result in the life they desire.

the life I want...
Hopeful Kids define what they want to accomplish in life in the form of positive goals, then they initiate choices to achieve those goals.

through positive choices and goals.

Hopeful Kids are focused on positive choices and goals that will support what they want out of life. They take responsibility for their actions by ensuring their choices are in line with their positive goals. This guides their behavior toward positive results.

Obviously, a young person does not become hopeful overnight. Becoming hopeful is a process, not an event. The process requires choice, commitment and practice. That is the purpose of this program: to help you instill hope in your child through time commitments, positive choices, lots of practice, and, most important, love. I strongly believe that by committing yourself to this process, someday soon your children will discover their personal power and become Hopeful Kids.

Becoming a Hopeful Parent

Hopeful Kids come from Hopeful Parents! This program is grounded in this simple cause-and-effect truth.

Hope is an expectation or belief in the fulfillment of something positive. When hope is cultivated, it will grow and flourish. With proper care, reinforcement, modeling, and a healthy dose of love, a person learns to be hopeful. Yes, we learn to be hopeful. In general, children learn how to be hopeful from the most powerful influences in their lives: parents. Hopeful Parents are the examples by which their kids learn to be hopeful. And, when young people are full of hope they are less likely to get caught up in hopeless behavior. They have learned from their parents that they have the personal power to create the life they want through their positive choices and goals.

Sadly, many parents never learned to be hopeful because they themselves lacked examples when they were younger. If that describes you, this program can also help you to become full of hope. Remember, kids learn to be hopeful from Hopeful Parents. In recognition of this irrefutable truth, you will learn to become a Hopeful Parent by using this program and by being an example of hope. You have already begun to create a fertile environment that promotes hope by involving yourself in this program and by believing that you can help your child create a better life. Because of this, you are well on your way to becoming a Hopeful Parent and developing a Hopeful Kid.

It's okay if you don't feel hopeful right now. You didn't embark on HOPEFUL because you and your kids are already full of hope. Remember, becoming hopeful is a journey marked by work, time, and commitment. By committing yourself to this journey, you will reach your destination sooner than you think. In the meantime, though, it is vital that you act hopeful. Yes, act hopeful even if you don't feel hopeful. Acting differently leads to change. It is well established that by acting a certain way, good or bad, leads to adopting the acted behavior as a genuine habit. So by constantly acting hopeful, you will become hopeful.

You are probably asking yourself this question right now: "How can I begin to act hopeful if I don't feel hopeful?" The answer is positively simple. Hopeful people believe they can create the life they want through positive choices and goals. By focusing on this one word, positive, you can start acting hopeful today. Start by recognizing the positive qualities you offer your child: time, honesty, support, inspiration, courage, dependability, patience, and, most important, an unending supply of love. Next find and recognize the positive qualities your child possesses: the ability to make good choices, goal-focused effort, humor, honesty, the desire to have a better life, helpfulness around the house, assertiveness, imagination, commitment, good grades, athletic or artistic talent, and love for your family. If these ideas don't ring a bell, create your own list by identifying anything positive in yourself and your child.

In short, you can begin to act hopeful by seeing the positive qualities in your child, hearing the positive words your child speaks, speaking more positively, noticing the positive elements around you, and by being positive about your capacity to help your child and yourself achieve a better life. Commit yourself right now to paying attention to and reinforcing these positive qualities in your child, yourself, and your life with words, praise, and heartfelt action. Do this positive strategy for the next thirty days in a row, then determine for yourself if this positive way of acting and living causes you to feel and be more hopeful. It really is that positively simple!

Hopeful Principles

Your primary mission is to develop your son or daughter into a Hopeful Kid. You will accomplish this mission with solid objectives, strategies, and actions.

Hopeful revolves around seven key principles. In summary, here is what each letter represents as a principle.

H	Hour
O	Open
P	Purpose
E	Example
F	Find
U	Understand
L	Love

Each principle has one or two objectives. These are supported by a variety of strategies that illuminate the path of action that will lead to the accomplishment.

As you read each chapter, look for boxes that give you the opportunity to interact with the material and think through how it applies to your family. "At My House ..." encourages you to reflect on the relationships and experiences that have shaped you and how they affect your relationship with your children. "Hopeful Hour Tips" give you ideas for how to help your children learn and process key concepts. Then at the end of each chapter, you'll find some simple assignments to make sure you're absorbing the strategies and following through. Last, you'll find a planning section for each chapter. This is largely blank because it is up to you to put feet to the strategies and accomplish them within the context of your family. You'll carry out strategies during Hopeful Hour family times (see Chapter Three), so use this planning guide to make the best use of your family times.

No two families will do HOPEFUL in the same way. It's up to you to figure out what works with your kids. The ages and levels of maturity of your kids will guide you on how much time you spend on each principle or each strategy. Don't rush the process. Make sure your kids grasp each concept before going on to the next one. At the same time, realize that you will be circling back to previous principles to reinforce them and give your kids ample opportunities to master them—and to master and model them yourself.

Please keep in mind that as you read the contents of this book, it is important that you do your best to pay attention and complete all of the simple assignments. This hands-on approach will give you a greater understanding of the program and a higher level of comfort in implementing your action plan. It is recommended that you read the entire book to have the big picture of the seven key principles. Then you can go back to the first principle and begin teaching HOPEFUL to your kids. Look for frequent opportunities to create a new dimension in your relationship with your kids—a dimension of hope. I also suggest that you get yourself and each of your children a spiral notebook to document your journey and to keep track of the assignments you and your kids will need to complete as part of this program. This will serve as a workbook. Call it the Hopeful Kid Notebook, and every time there's an assignment or strategy activity, grab the notebook so you have a complete record of your family's HOPEFUL learning.

MAKE IT YOURS

Taken as a whole, *HOPEFUL KIDS* offers the most effective methods for inspiring hope in a young person. That said, however, this program is not intended to be a rigid prescription for doing this one specific way. Instead, it is intended to be a flexible approach that offers a variety of strategies within a systematic framework to accomplish the same mission: develop a Hopeful Kid. Although the goal will always be the same, the way or how you will go about it will not. What works best for one child may not work for another. Also, there is no specific timetable that determines when a young person should become hopeful. It is totally dependent upon the needs of the child—not the clock.

Armed with this understanding, subscribe to the belief that experimentation, trial-and-error, and good old-fashioned hard work will be your best travel companions on this marvelous adventure. Practically speaking, I recommend that you work and experiment with everything within this system, then determine what works best for your child. Do this and eventually you will discover that special mixture of strategies that will guide you and your child to a successful completion of your mission. When this happens, and it will, you will have given your youngster the best gift ever—the gift of life.

By choosing to use HOPEFUL KIDS, you have taken the first and most important step toward reclaiming your sons and daughters from a hopeless, lifeless future. Because of this conscious, positive choice, you have begun to change. You have started to act differently. You have started to act hopefully. You have chosen life—for yourself, for your kids, for your family.

One last thing before we continue: This program provides all the knowledge, help, tools, directions, inspiration, and strategies you will need to guide you and your child to become hopeful. In short, HOPEFUL provides everything your family will need to successfully complete this journey except four vital ingredients. Without them, this program will not work. The good news is, each of these four ingredients is at your immediate disposal and is ready to be enlisted for action right now. Here they are: parent, child, time, and commitment.

That's it. This may seem rather obvious, but without you, your child, your time, and your commitment, there is no journey to becoming hopeful. Since you have made it this far, it is safe to assume that you have given these last essential ingredients. Good job! You are ready to resume your journey to becoming a Hopeful Parent and developing a Hopeful Kid.

There you have it. *HOPEFUL KIDS* seems simple because it is simple. Bear in mind this is just the skeleton; we will add flesh to these bones in the upcoming sections of this book.

Okay, roll up your sleeves and put on your thinking caps. Here we go!

CHAPTER 3

Principle 1: Hour

Objective 1: Invest one hour of hope in your child per month.

"Time is money." That familiar expression demonstrates the value we put on our time—it's worth something, it can generate rewards for us, we can use it to get things we want. Imagine someone gave you the gift of a debit card with a fixed amount of time on it. Would you spend it willy-nilly, figuring there is more where that came from, or would you think carefully about how to spend your time to get the best value? We do truly spend time. We don't have an unending supply, and that reality gives time its value.

When you get right down to it, without time there can be no life. Once your time runs out, your life ceases. Hence, it is easy to understand that when we speak of life and time together, we call it a lifetime.

Our time is limited because our time accounts are limited. Each of us has his own lifetime to spend his time as he chooses. We can spend time wisely or unwisely. It is up to us individually. How we spend our time demonstrates our priorities; when you add up the time you spend doing any one activity, you realize what really matters to you most. Just as important, how you spend your time communicates strongly to those around you, especially your children, what is most important to you. Hmm ... this really makes you think about how you actually spend your time.

Obviously, in light of this, time is your most valuable commodity. No "thing" is more valuable. Time is worth much more than any amount of money, including gold or diamonds. It follows, then, that if you have time, you are truly wealthy, because anything worth more than all the currency, gems, and precious metals in the world makes you rich. And to think you believed being a millionaire was a big deal. Not anymore. Ask any millionaire, or billionaire for that matter, what is the one thing that can't be bought? Time!

ONE HOUR A MONTH

When you spend time with your children, you are investing in their lives and their potential. By sharing your most valuable commodity with them, you are sending this most important message: "I love you. You are my number one priority." This is why time is the bedrock of the HOPEFUL process and why it is so crucial to the development of hope. There is, and can be, no better investment of your precious, limited time.

Respecting this irrefutable fact, HOPEFUL will require you to invest one hour of hope in your child per month. That's it—just one hour per month. You can accomplish this several ways.

1. Add this valuable hour into your family routine. Find an hour when the whole family is usually home and available. If variable work schedules make this hard, then look ahead every couple

of months and identify time slots you think will be available. Schedule in your Hopeful Hour for one of these times.

2. If one hour on a predictable basis seems unrealistic for the schedules in your household, spend two thirty-minute sessions over two days per month (e.g., Wednesday evening 6 p.m. to 6:30 p.m. and Saturday afternoon 2 p.m. to 2:30 p.m.).

3. Perhaps your family schedule truly is chaotic enough that you can't establish when you'll have an hour together on a regular basis. Perhaps one parent's work schedule changes weekly or involves out-of-town travel. As soon as you know these variable factors, sit down with a calendar and identify each month's hour. If you can predict only a week or two out, that's okay, as long as you are consistent about finding the hour.

4. Look for smaller segments and unusual places. For instance, you might know that you'll spend twenty minutes in the car together going to soccer practice and games three times a week. Be purposeful about using those twenty minutes. Maybe you walk the dog together in the evenings—or could, if you planned it. Maybe you drive to church a half an hour from your home. If you are intentional about any of these times, you can use them for the Hopeful program.

Some activities in the chapters that follow do require a concentrated sit-down-and-talk approach to use paper and pencil for a specific task. Others are more fluid. A Hopeful Strategy might be to have a conversation about a certain idea, and this can be done anywhere. An assignment might be to exhibit an attitude for your kids, and it will be up to you to identify the opportunities to do this.

You decide which approach will work best based on your family's needs. The point is to be intentional, thoughtful, and purposeful. Instead of throwing a DVD in to keep the kids quiet in the car, use the time for a planned discussion. Talk about a question you've decided in advance to bring up.

Also, if you have more than one child, you will need to determine if it is more beneficial to work with your kids together or separately. That said, however, I recommend that you work with your children together. In addition to being an efficient use of your precious time, it is the best way to promote family bonding and learning. You'll develop a common language that the whole family can use in future problem-solving and relational glitches.

A University of Michigan study released in 2001 revealed that children between the ages of three and twelve spent on average 120 hours a month with their mothers and more than 90 hours per month with their fathers. HOPEFUL asks for only one of those hours per month on a structured basis to accomplish your mission.

Remember, how you choose to spend your time reveals your priorities. Choose to spend it with your children and you are powerfully communicating to them, "I love you. You are my number one priority." This is the wisest investment of your time. Eventually this investment will pay huge dividends for a lifetime.

HOUR STRATEGIES

HOUR Strategy 1: *Create a Hopeful Hour for your children.*

Identify and commit at least one hour per month to instilling hope in your children by using this program. The simplest way to do this is to look at your family schedule and decide what potential times and days would be best for spending this hopeful time together—then commit yourself to dedicate this time to the HOPEFUL program.

If your kids are busy with sports, ballet, friends, Scouts, or other activities, get their input, because this will affect their routines. However, it is best to have a schedule in mind before you talk with them. Ask what they think, but remember you are the one creating the schedule, not your kids. As parents, you know what is best for them. Scheduling time to help them become hopeful is definitely in their best interest. Make sure you emphasize how important this time together is to them and to you. You can rest assured that no matter what changes or sacrifices you have to make to create this schedule, the benefits will always outweigh the costs. Remember this: children are highly resilient and adaptive. Thus, create the schedule and they will learn to accept and adjust to it.

Teenagers, by nature, want their independence in preparation for adulthood. Respecting this coming-of-age reality, be particularly sensitive in carving out this hour with teens. Do not expect immediate enthusiasm. Also, do not tell them you just want this time "to talk." As parents, you know that requesting time to talk is tantamount to throwing up a brick wall. Worse yet, it is the surest way to invoke teenage paranoia and a prolonged bout of lockjaw.

Try this strategy instead. Find a casual moment with your teen and say something like this:

> I've noticed how quickly you're growing up and how time seems to be flying by. Before you are all grown up, I would like to find a little time, just one hour per month, to stay in touch with you and catch up on things.

At this point, your teen may think you are crazy. That's okay. Parents are supposed to be crazy in the eyes of a hormone-possessed teen. Despite this, be tenacious and firm about getting your teenager to commit to one hour per month, whether it's all at one time or in twenty-minute segments. Teens know when their parents are serious about something. Be serious about this! Make this hopeful time together a top priority. You are the parent, and you have the responsibility for raising and protecting your kids. Thus, even if your teen does not see the benefit of committing to this scheduled time initially, make it happen anyway! This may be the last time you will have to guide your teen to becoming hopeful before he or she is independent in this confusing, destructive world. Keep this idea in the forefront of your thinking, and you will surely find a way to spend time together.

Once you have created this schedule, commit your family to adhering to it. As expected, there will be days when this will not be possible due to unexpected events. No big deal. Just get back on track as soon as possible. However, if this continues to happen, then look for another time slot that better meets the needs of your family. The most important thing is to get into the habit of spending these hours of hope together as a family, because time is an essential ingredient in becoming hopeful. Lead by example and your kids will follow.

HOUR Strategy 2: *Create value for your Hopeful Hour.*

Kids look forward to being with their parents when it makes them feel better about themselves and the world they live in. Building on this fact, create value for this Hopeful Hour by underscoring that it is designed to help them feel better and have a better life. And if the title "Hopeful Hour" isn't your cup of tea, call it "Family Time" or anything else you want that will work for your family. You might even invite kids to be creative in naming this time together. The name isn't important; making a commitment to spending this time together doing this program is.

Create value for this time together by emphasizing your desire to help your kids deal with the confusion and complexities of life as well as the eventual decisions they will have to make about the future. Keep in mind that teenagers are closer to this point than younger kids. No matter what you say, keep it simple, honest, and to the point. Being intentional about what you want to do during this time adds value and keeps kids from wondering what the point is. When you begin having Hopeful Hours, you can assure kids that you will have an agenda; you won't be sitting around the family room staring at each other and wondering what to say. Set the example of being the one to take initiative during this hour and soon your kids won't be so shocked that you actually want to listen to them. Give this value-added strategy your best effort and you will soon discover that your children will look forward to these hopeful hours more than any other time you spend with them.

At My House

> My kids would think Hopeful Hour has value if …
>
> _____
>
> _____
>
> _____
>
> _____
>
> _____

Hour Strategy 3: *Dedicate all your Hopeful Hours to completing all of the strategies of* Hopeful.

Given the typical family's weekly schedule, you are probably involved in all kinds of activities with your kids: playing games, cooking and eating, doing homework and housework, watching television, communicating, going to church, participating in sports and hobbies, resolving differences, praying, sorting laundry, cleaning the litter box, traveling, and any number of other family activities. Families spend time together doing family stuff. Every family is unique in how they "hang out." Respecting this basic truth, Hopeful encourages your family to continue doing whatever positive activities you do together—with one important exception: the inclusion of the one hour per month you are engaged in this program. This time is different, and it requires a higher degree of commitment and diligence. Of all the time your family spends together, dedicate this Hopeful Hour to completing all of the strategies of Hopeful. Use this time for one purpose only: developing Hopeful Kids. In each chapter, you'll find strategies that change how you approach various situations and conversations. As you absorb and begin to use new relational skills, your kids will follow your example. The Hopeful Hour is a time when you intentionally look for ways to pass these strategies on to your kids. It is an hour with a purpose; use it for that purpose only.

MEET THE WILSON FAMILY

Carl and Tina Wilson have two children: Jimmy, age nine, and Sam, age eleven. The family's schedule is hectic with both parents working full-time and both children active with friends and sports. Carl works as a bus driver, while Tina is a medical assistant. Tina likens their busy lifestyle to a beehive with everyone buzzing around trying to get from one place to the other. According to Carl, he gets off work from driving a bus all day only to start his second job as a taxicab driver for his kids. Sound familiar?

After learning about HOPEFUL, the parents both agreed to be involved in the program. They also decided to work with Jimmy and Sam together rather than apart. This, they felt, was more in line with their values and schedule. Plus, they were confident the boys would benefit more from the program this way. To begin, they looked over their weekly schedule to find potential days and times when they could schedule one hour of hope per month. Things were complicated because Carl was required to be on call for work every other Saturday, and the boys had ball practice several days of the week and games nearly every weekend. Also, the parents bowled on Wednesday evenings, and Tina was enrolled in a psychology class at the community college on Monday nights. Additionally, they always attended church on Sunday mornings.

Once the parents could see their whole schedule, they immediately knew it would be challenging to reprioritize even one hour of their precious time. However, where there's a will, there's a way. They definitely had the will; they just had to find the way. Clearly, there would have to be some sacrifices, but they knew the costs were worth the benefits. After talking about various options, they created a draft schedule and agreed to go over it with Jimmy and Sam the following day after dinner. Because of Carl and Tina's strong commitment to family, they decided to call this time together "Family Time."

After Jimmy and Sam cleared the dishes from the table, Carl and Tina told their sons they had something important to discuss. They began by explaining the value of spending time together as a family. Carl then said, "This time together, Family Time, is very important because it gives us a chance to stay in touch with you guys and to help you create the life you want." The parents went on to point out how they felt they needed to create more time together because, in Tina's words, "We love you guys very much, and you are our number one priority." Before showing the draft schedule, the parents stressed how important it was for everyone to work together to make this happen.

During the first fifteen minutes, the boys raised a couple of concerns based on their desire to stay in sports and hang out with their friends. In an understanding tone, Carl reminded the boys that there would have to be some sacrifices because, as he put it, "Family Time is the most important time." Next, Tina showed her two sons how she and Carl had made some sacrifices in their schedules to make this happen. Specifically, she pointed out how she had readjusted her school and Bible-study schedule, while Carl had reorganized his workout and grocery-shopping schedule.

For the next half hour, the family discussed potential changes, moving things around and listening to the boys' recommendations on how they could readjust their active schedules: sports, homework, chores, television, buddy time, and playtime. In the last fifteen minutes of this hour, the family agreed to the following Family Time Schedule: Every other Tuesday, 6 p.m. to 7 p.m.

The Wilsons decided to schedule two hours of Family Time per month rather than one because of their desire to commit more time to HOPEFUL. They all agreed that this schedule allowed the family to continue most of the positive activities they were already involved in with minimal changes. Finally, in anticipation of any scheduling conflicts or setbacks, the family agreed to immediately get back on track if they missed a session. Before finishing, the parents once again underscored the importance of dedicating Family Time to helping Jimmy and Sam create the life they wanted. Next, they put the schedule to paper and posted it on the fridge. They found great comfort in knowing they had completed the first strategy of HOPEFUL by creating a solid time-foundation for developing their sons into Hopeful Kids. Now it was just a matter of time—one hour at a time.

SMALL INVESTMENT, BIG RETURN

As you invest these hours of hope in your children, you should see some positive changes. For starters, you should observe an increased desire to participate in the program. For some youth, this Hopeful Hour or Family Time, or whatever you choose to name it will become one of their most anticipated and cherished times with you. Gradually you will notice how this time of hope will positively influence the other time your family spends together. Also, your kids will begin to perceive this investment of time as a statement of importance. That is to say, through your actions and time commitments you are boldly claiming that you love them, that they are important to you and that they really matter. When you make your kids important to you, they in turn, become important to themselves; they start to feel better about themselves and their lives. This sets into motion the process that leads to a positive self-esteem and an optimistic outlook on life—in one word, hopeful. Considering this awesome outcome, it truly is remarkable how such a small investment of time can result in such a gigantic return for a lifetime.

With this in mind, the rest of this book is dedicated to showing you what to do during these hours of hope in order to achieve your mission: Develop Hopeful Kids.

HOUR ASSIGNMENTS

It is vital that you make a commitment to completing all of the simple assignments contained in this book. They will bolster your confidence and hone your skills in developing Hopeful Kids. Consequently, make this commitment and you will reap the rewards: sons and daughters who are full of hope, full of life. Keep the Hopeful Kid's Notebooks handy to help everyone stay focused on the value of your Hopeful Hours.

Okay, crack your knuckles and recharge your thinking caps. Here we go.

HOUR Assignment 1: *Analyze your time.*

Not including work, list the top three areas where you spend the most time. Look at your daily schedule and conduct a time-allotment assessment to determine your time priorities. "Work" is considered time committed to providing for your family. While it may be your biggest time commitment, it is not your first priority, so for purposes of this exercise, we'll exclude the time you spend making a living. However, if you are working fifty hours or more per week, and this is detracting you from the time you should be spending with your kids, it is time to reprioritize your time. Remember: your kids are your most important work and time investment!

1. _____

2. _____

3. _____

4. _____

5. _____

Hour Assignment 2: *Make sure kids are at the top of the list.*

If your children are at the top of the list, pat yourself on the back and go to Assignment 3. If your children are not at the top of the list, get them there! Reprioritize your time to make them your number one investment of time. It's possible you can spend time with your kids at the same time you do other things, but are you just dragging them along because they're too young to stay home alone, or are you also engaging them in meaningful ways while you go about errands, shopping, meal preparation, and so on?

Below, briefly state how you will go about achieving this most important objective. If circumstances beyond your control prevent you from doing this right now, state what they are and how you will go about resolving each of them as soon as possible so that you can make your children your number one investment of time. As you complete this assignment, keep this in mind: Schedules can be compromised, not children.

Making Sure my Kids are at the Top of my List...

1. _____

2. _____

3. _____

4. _____

Hour Assignment 3: *Plan whether to work with kids individually or together.*

If you have one child, go to Assignment 4. If you have more than one child, determine if it is best to work with your children together or separately. Once more, I recommend that you work with your children together because of efficiency and family bonding. For example, you will have to commit one hour total per month if you work with your children together. However, if you decide to work with your children separately, you will have to invest one hour per child per month (i.e., two kids equals two hours per month, three kids equals three hours per month). That is why I recommend you work with them together rather than separately. At the same time, there are valid reasons for working with kids separately: they may be too far apart in age, one may be mature enough to progress more quickly through the Hopeful activities, and so on. Determine which approach works best for your family.

My Plan for Making my Kids my #1 Investment of Time...

_____

_____

_____

_____

_____

_____

_____

Hour Assignment 4: *Identify potential sacrifices.*

You learned earlier that, on the average, parents spend at least 120 hours per month with their children. Chances are, then, that you already spend enough time with your kids. Now all you have to do is reprioritize one of these 120 hours (less than one percent) to complete Hopeful. If this seems difficult, spend some time really thinking about and searching for

one potential hour of time you are willing to sacrifice to make HOPEFUL
work for your family. Look at every time slot in your schedule that could
be replaced with an hour of hope. Remember: be the first to sacrifice.
Below, list one potential hour of time you could reprioritize in your
family's schedule for this program per month:

Identify your Potential Sacrifices...

1. _____

2. _____

3. _____

4. _____

5. _____

HOUR Assignment 5: *Find your family's Hopeful Hour.*

Gather your family and discuss the best options for finding one hour a
month to spend together learning to be hopeful. Write here when you
will meet with your family.

Find your Family's Hopeful Hour...

_____

_____

_____

_____

_____

_____

Hopeful Hour Planning Page

Write in your own words the main substance of Principle 1: Hour.

```
_____

_____

_____
```

Plan how many Hopeful Hours you think you'll need to devote to this principle. List the dates you will have these Hopeful Hours. Jot down a key activity you will use in each Hopeful Hour to engage your children in learning the principle.

Your activities may be suggestions you find in the chapter or adaptations you know your child will enjoy. Make sure your plan includes all the key strategies of the principle. Continue on an additional sheet of paper if necessary.

	Date	Strategy	Key Activity

CHAPTER 4

Principle 2: OPEN

Objective 2: Be open with your child.

Finding one hour a month to instill hope in your children is the first practical step of the HOPEFUL program. Now comes the part where you might have to change more than your schedule; you might have to change yourself. Being open with children is essential to forming loving and trusting relationships. Without openness there can be no meaningful relationship—only coexistence. But being open often calls for self-examination and being willing to take risks.

People are "open" when they receive, respect, and respond to others. They exude a willingness to listen and talk without pretense. Words and phrases like real, sincere, straightforward, and easy to talk to generally capture the essence of an open person. As expected, parents are a potent force in helping their children learn how to be open. Yes, just as kids learn how to be hopeful, they also learn how to be open from parents who intently listen, honestly express themselves, and encourage the same in return. In short, open parents create open kids.

That said, pay attention to this truth: Kids are adept at figuring out when a person is not being open with them. With each insincere interaction, their confidence in that individual incrementally deteriorates. If this occurs repeatedly, they learn not to go to that person for advice or help. Should this be a parent, the results are predictably tragic. Knowing this, parents must be open with their children by genuinely receiving, respecting, and responding to them and their needs. Equally as important, an open parent encourages and promotes a similar response. Children learn to be open by seeing openness in action.

If this open style of communication describes you, this principle of HOPEFUL will sharpen your skills. However, if this is difficult for you, as is the case with many parents, don't despair. You can learn how to be open by applying and adopting the forthcoming OPEN Strategies. Practicing them will make you more comfortable with them. And best of all, through your example, your kids will learn to be open with you. Therefore, there can only be one right decision: Be open with your kids.

OPEN STRATEGIES

OPEN Strategy 1: *Be the first to influence your children by making them your first priority.*

Kids are more willing to be open with their parents if they know they are their parents' first priority. You have already learned that making your kids your number one time investment is a powerful method for communicating this message. Similarly, to foster openness, you must be willing to make yourself available when your children need you. Keep this in mind: If you don't make time to help your kids, someone else will. Should this be the unfortunate result, chances are great this other person will not have the same vested interest in helping your son or daughter in the same manner as you would. It is this clear cut: You or someone else? Your priorities, as evidenced by your actions, not your words, ultimately will reveal what is most important to you and to your kids.

To successfully implement this strategy, all you have to say to your sons and daughters is this simple yet powerful sentence: "I will make time for you if you need me." Make sure your kids understand that the word need means that they need your help right now. It is important that you tell them this because when they use the word need, it will require you to bring to a halt whatever you are doing. Continue by telling your children that all they ever have to say to you to make this happen are three simple words: "I need you." When you hear these words, you will know that it is something crucial, and you will make time to listen and to help.

HOPEFUL HOUR TIP

In one of your first Hopeful Hours, make sure your kids know they can count on you. Answer their questions about what constitutes need and talk about some examples that may come up in your family.

Make your children your first priority when it comes to your time and you will be the first person they will turn to. This gives you the advantage of being the first person to help and influence them. This is a powerful position to be in because the person who is given the first opportunity to influence a hurt and confused young person has a tremendous effect on that young person's eventual decision. Here is what it boils down to: Make your children your first priority and they will give you the first opportunity to help them during times of need.

OPEN Strategy 2: *Be willing to talk with your son or daughter about anything, anytime, anywhere—no limits!*

"No limits." These are the last two words parents want to hear when it comes to their children. When combined in the same sentence, no limits and kids induce gut-wrenching, heart-pounding anxiety in even the most liberal parent. Every parent knows that age-appropriate, reasonable boundaries must be defined and maintained to ensure children are protected and grow up with a strong sense of right and wrong. Conversely, when it comes to fostering and modeling open communication with your kids, there can be no limits—absolutely none. Whenever you place limits around what your children can and cannot talk about, openness immediately begins to wane. This suppressive approach guarantees that young people will seek the advice of someone else when they need help. If this other person has less than honorable intentions, matters will only get worse. To prevent this from happening to your children, you must be open to helping them deal with issues related to violence, suicide, drugs, death, sex, racism, rape, puberty, anger, homosexuality, birth control, God, and anything else that concerns them. This is the true nature of being open.

HOPEFUL HOUR TIP

You may be thinking of some areas of your life that you wouldn't want to talk about with your kids. Anticipate ahead of time what these might be and plan how you will respond in a way that is open and honest while respectful of experiences that may be painful for you or someone else. While no topic is out of bounds, use wisdom in discerning what information is appropriate to share.

Ideally parents would begin practicing open communication with their son or daughter from day one. If for whatever reason this has not happened, it is never too late to start. The invitation begins with these words:

> I really care about you and what is going on in your life. So whatever you need to talk with me about, no matter what it is, I will be there for you. Just let me know with these words: "I need you."

Since this may be the first time your children have heard these heartfelt words from you, don't expect an immediate outpouring of emotion. It will take time for them to believe you really mean what you say. They will undoubtedly expect you to back it up with substance— deeds over words. As a result, prepare yourself to be tested. No matter what, pass each and every test for this basic reason: Open, no-limits communication gives you a tremendous advantage for being the first person to influence your children when confusion, stress, or sadness cause them to be highly impressionable to the input of others. Any discomfort you may feel about doing this is a small price to pay when you consider the alternative: no control or input when children are most vulnerable. Since this is the last thing you want, make the invitation, pass every test, and start being open with your kids by proving that you are willing to talk about anything, anytime, anywhere—no limits!

Open Strategy 3: *Risk first. Take the first step to being open by admitting your fears.*

You can't very well have open communication if you limit what your children can and cannot discuss. If this open, no-limits style of communication causes you to feel uncomfortable because of any fears you may have with respect to embarrassment, a lack of knowledge or whatever else that may be raising your temperature, you need to realize that all you ever have to do to get the ball rolling is one thing: admit your fears. By admitting your fears to your kids, you have risked first and courageously demonstrated that you can be open with them. See this as an opportunity rather than a problem. This sincere statement will give you an idea of how to get started:

> You mean everything to me. Because of this, I know it is important that we are open with each other. To be honest, I am a little nervous about how to do this. I am admitting this because I want you to know that I am willing to talk with you about anything, no matter what it is, so I can help you if you need me. So from this point forward, if you ever need me, just let me know by telling me, "I need you," and I will make the time to be there for you, anytime, anywhere.

Upon making this statement, keep the momentum going by asking your child this question: "Do you feel okay about being open with me?" If your child says yes, then see what happens next; keep being open. If your child says no, then gently persist by being open whenever the opportunity arises. An older child or teen may have more trouble opening up than a younger child, particularly if there have been negative experiences with being open. Again, don't expect miracles the first time around. Prepare to be tested time and time again. Consistently back up your words with genuine action.

Get over any fears you may harbor about this type of open, no-limits communication, because your fears pale in comparison to the fears your child may be feeling and want to discuss. Do whatever it takes to make yourself practice this with your kids: struggle, embarrass yourself, stick your foot in your mouth, cry, laugh hysterically, stumble over your words, but do it because the payoff is huge—open kids who will give you the first opportunity to help them when they are vulnerable.

OPEN Strategy 4: *Be more open by paying attention to your body language and voice tone.*

Most of what we communicate to others is done without words. In fact, most communication experts believe that 75 percent to 90 percent of what we convey to others comes through our body language and voice tone. That is why we sometimes find it difficult to understand what the other person is "really saying" when we are reading a letter or electronically interacting (e-mailing and texting) with others. Understandably, this form of communication results in the highest level of misunderstanding and miscommunication. The reason for this is simple: We can't see or hear the other person. Consequently, the best way to openly communicate with others is through face-to-face interaction. And since this is how we most often interact with our immediate family, especially during our Hopeful Hours, when we feel the need to be open we will concentrate on this form of personal communication. Now let's see how body language and voice tone affect face-to-face communication.

In a nutshell, here is how it works. The greater the continuity between our verbal (spoken words and voice tone) and nonverbal communication (body language), the greater the probability the receiver will understand our intended message. Said simply, how we say something is more important than what we say.

Suppose a teenage boy returns from an evening with his friends. His mother is sitting in the living room as he enters the house. He sees his mother but does not speak and hurries toward his bedroom. As he passes his mother, she asks: "How was your evening?" With arms folded, eyes looking down, biting his lower lip and nervously tapping his foot, he answers in a distressed voice: "Fine. No problems."

It doesn't take a genius to realize there is more to this situation than what is being revealed verbally. This example clearly demonstrates how body language and voice tone can communicate much more about what is really going on than words alone. But what if the mother does not look up as the boy speaks? What if she only takes in his literal words?

With this in mind, here are some easy-to-remember tactics that will help you to be a more open and effective face-to-face communicator with your sons and daughters:

- Ask yourself this question while you are communicating face-to-face with your kids: "Does my body language and voice tone match what I am saying?"
- Focus on what is being said—truly listen.
- Uncross your legs and arms and lean toward your child.
- Demonstrate you are listening and interested by paying attention.
- Maintain eye contact and facial expressions that fit the situation.
- Speak in a tone that fits your feelings and message.

We significantly enhance the quality, power, and accuracy of a message by aligning and paying attention to our body language, voice tone, and spoken words. More important, however, we greatly improve the likelihood that our message will be understood. And this, more than anything else, is the ultimate goal of communication. Learn and model this type of integrated communication and you will significantly improve openness and understanding in your family.

Hopeful Hour Tip

When you talk about open communication with your kids, practice interpreting nonverbal language. Take turns showing facial expressions or postures that illustrate a variety of feelings while the others try to guess the feeling. Discuss the importance of keeping verbal and non-verbal communication in sync.

OPEN Strategy 5: *Teach openness by practicing the three R's: Receive, Respect, Respond.*

We have all heard of the three R's as they relate to school: Reading, 'Riting, and 'Rithmetic. Well, now you have three R's to remember when it comes to being open with others, especially your children: Receive, Respect, and Respond.

The process of open communication begins with receiving your child. Receiving is best accomplished by inviting and welcoming your child when he or she wants to talk with you. This would include making a sincere invitation to talk with you about anything whenever the need arises. When your son or daughter makes this request, you would immediately, or as soon as circumstances permit, make time to listen and help by focusing on the child's needs.

Next, open communication requires you to respect a child as a separate person with his or her own opinions and views. Respect requires you to accept who the child is and what the child has to say, even though you may not agree. The mere fact that you are willing to take the time to listen goes a long way toward cultivating respect. This is respect in action.

At some point, your child will probably want you to respond with advice or feedback. Responding is most effective when it is honest, nonjudgmental, and emotionally in sync with the situation. This is easily accomplished, as you already know, by ensuring that your words are matched to your body language and tone. If there is a discrepancy between your verbal and nonverbal response, mixed messages will result.

For example, a father is watching TV when his teenage daughter suddenly enters the room sobbing and declares, "My life is not worth living ever since I broke up with Rob." While still watching TV and eating potato chips, he casually remarks, "Don't worry about it. There are plenty more boyfriends where he came from. You'll be fine." In this situation, his verbal response will not be taken seriously because his nonverbal language and tone are loudly proclaiming, "I don't really care!" And as you have probably already surmised, this father just lost his opportunity to be the first person to influence his daughter while she is desperate and vulnerable. This is a recipe for disaster.

Instead, do your best to receive, respect, and respond to your children. This is the essence of open communication. Practice, teach, and continually reinforce the three R's of communication with your kids and they will give you the first opportunity to help them before making any life-changing decisions.

At My House

My kids will know I'm really paying attention when I ...

_____

_____

_____

_____

OPEN Strategy 6. *Take Ten and Think–Choose–Act. Teach and practice these strategies whenever you or your child feels upset.*

Sometimes our feelings consume us. We can't always choose how we feel, but we can always choose how we will respond to our feelings. Every action is a choice. However, before we choose a particular action, we have to think about it first. Even when people say, "I wasn't thinking about it, I just did it," there was some mental activity in the brain before the body or mouth responded. The brain gives the order, and the body and mouth follow that order. Without the order, there can be no words or actions.

The human brain works at speeds that make a computer look like a snail. We process information faster than we can comprehend. Given this, it is not surprising that many people mistakenly believe they are at the mercy of some mysterious force that causes them to do something automatically without thinking about it first. It just seems that way because we are unaware of the cognition before the ignition. In most instances we are only conscious of the act itself, not the analysis that goes on behind the scenes. Once more, this happens because we think and process so quickly. The linear process follows three specific steps in exactly this order: Think–Choose–Act. In all cases, thinking takes place before choosing or acting. We are all endowed with the ability to think before we choose to act—always. Think about it!

Granted, there are those times when this fact of life does not seem to apply. Things just seem to happen with no thought whatsoever. The most obvious example of this is when we are overcome with emotion, especially when we are upset. During these emotionally consuming moments we are most prone to saying and doing things we don't mean. Consider this case in point: An angry teenage boy tells his father, "I hate you!" after his driving privileges have been suspended for staying out past curfew. Caught up in the moment, the father responds in a like fashion: "You'll be lucky if you ever see the inside of a car again. Get out of my sight!" As expected, it only gets worse from there.

All of this disturbing and unnecessary emotional energy could have been easily avoided if either the teenage boy or father had simply realized he was angry, stepped back mentally from the situation for a moment, taken in some deep breaths, and thought about what he was going to do next. That is what the Take Ten strategy is designed to do: create a ten-second timeout from the stressful event at hand so people can become conscious of their thinking before they choose an action. By taking a little time to think and relax, reactions are more likely to be reasonable. In other words, when a distressing moment arises, all we ever have to do to prevent it from escalating to an angry, unproductive shouting match is to Take Ten by following these simple guidelines:

- Say you are upset and that you need to take some time to think.
- Do and say nothing for at least ten seconds. Relax.
- Remind yourself that only you can choose your next action.
- Think about and choose your options calmly and carefully.
- Take as much time as you need to regain control.
- Walk away if you don't feel in control.

Oftentimes doing nothing is your best reaction to a tense situation until things cool down. When things are really heated, your best option is to walk away. The idea here is that a little timeout is much more beneficial than an emotional break where unintended yet harmful verbal and/or physical outbursts result. Teach and practice this strategy the next time you or your child's emotional temperature starts to rise. You will quickly find out that a little time invested in saying and doing nothing when you are upset will return greatly when it comes to getting meaningful results a short time later.

AT MY HOUSE

> **Three things that tend to set me off are ...**
>
> _____
>
> _____
>
> _____
>
> _____

Answer this question honestly. Then during a Hopeful Hour, be the first to share your answer and invite others to acknowledge the things that set them off. Recognizing triggers is the first step to maintaining self-control.

Before we go on, it should be pointed out that in no way does "open, no-limits communication" give your child the excuse to speak to you in a profane or disrespectful manner. Granted, there will be those times when a kid will make a derogatory remark about you in the heat of the moment. As long as it is occasional, keep the flow going and ignore these emotional slips of the tongue. However, should tempers flare and the occasional becomes the norm, you need to take corrective action immediately. When you feel this is happening, say something like this:

> I don't appreciate the way you are talking to me right now. It sounds like you are upset. Do you need to Take Ten before we continue?

When you ask this question, give your child time to think and relax; don't push or rush. Be patient and wait until he or she makes a choice to continue or discontinue, then support the decision. Let your child experience the ability to think and choose actions (Think–Choose–Act) during times of emotional upheaval. If your child can do this with you, he or she will be able to do this with others when you aren't around.

The reverse is also true. If you feel that you are getting abnormally frustrated or angry, Take Ten. Also, in the event your child needs to Take Ten but refuses to do so after repeated invitations, then you should initiate the time break and return later when things have calmed down. This is often the case with young or emotionally charged kids. When you resume your discussion, take this opportunity to teach the importance of self-awareness, emotional control, and respect of others. Make sure to point out your willingness to support the child's choice to Take Ten—or however long is needed—when a child feels on edge, frustrated, or angry. Through your example and these open discussions, your kid will eventually learn how to recognize the need to take a break and return in better control.

HOPEFUL HOUR TIP

During a Hopeful Hour, share about a time when you lost your cool and should have remembered to Take Ten. This might have happened at work or at home. Use this as a chance to explain Take Ten. Talk about the benefits and how you will help each other use this strategy for more open communication.

Now let's say that you are having a difficult discussion with your son or daughter and things are really starting to escalate—screaming, shouting, outbursts, physical confrontations, and the like. If this is the case, both of you will need to take an extended break and agree to talk later. No matter what, though, take as much time as you need to get back in control! There is no reason to continue trying to openly communicate if you or your kid is acting and responding out of anger. Think about it and relax. Then come back to it when you are both in control of what you are saying and doing.

With that last thought in mind, the Take Ten approach is most effective when it is combined with this question: "Do I feel in control?" This is our next strategy.

OPEN Strategy 7: *Ask this question when you or your child feels angry: "Do I feel in control?"*

Angry people do regrettable things. This happens because angry people choose to let their agitated feelings dictate their thinking and actions. It is a simple fact of life that most people find it difficult to think straight when they feel upset. When emotions are surging, we can become slaves to our most destructive impulses. Too often this rage–react–regret cycle seriously damages or destroys relationships even though we apologize for our impulsive actions later. Most of the time, it is too little too late. That is the price we pay for allowing our fiery impulses to control us. The key to preventing this vicious cycle from negatively impacting your family is to be conscious of how much control you have when anger seizes you. One of the most practical strategies for doing this is to ask this one question when anger first rears its ugly head:

"Do I feel in control?"

If your answer is yes, continue working on the issue toward a positive resolution. If the answer is no, just as in Take Ten, say you are too upset and you need to take some time to calm down and think—and walk away immediately. To make this strategy most effective in a family system, everyone must agree to follow these five basic rules:

1.   Everyone in the family must agree to ask this question if he or she starts to feel angry or when strong feelings start to take over: "Do I feel in control?"

2.   If the person feels in control, the process of resolution can continue.

3.   If the person does not feel in control, the interaction must discontinue immediately and the upset person must be allowed to leave the situation.

4.   The upset person agrees to come back to the issue within 24 hours or when this person is back in control. This person agrees to tell someone what is going on if one day (24 hours) has elapsed since the time-out. No matter what, though, this person starts with a clean slate when interactions resume: Go back to the issue, not the anger.

5.   Anyone can ask this question if someone else appears to be getting out of control as a result of strong emotions: "Do you feel in control?" When this happens, rules 1 through 4 apply.

In the next strategy, you and your children will learn how to openly express your feelings even when you are upset.

HOPEFUL HOUR TIP

During a Hopeful Hour, take turns naming things that really bug you and may even cause you to lose control. Then talk about how to regain control by following the rules above.

OPEN Strategy 8: *Teach your children how to openly express their feelings by being assertive.*

One of the best ways for expressing positive or negative feelings is to be assertive. Being assertive means openly expressing one's feelings and needs without offending others. No matter what the feeling—happiness, anger, sadness, anxiety, love, sorrow, fear, disappointment, rejection, elation, failure, etc.—assertiveness offers a positive process for freely stating how we feel and how something or someone is favorably or unfavorably affecting us. Without question, it is the most powerful way to communicate our feelings when we feel angry. By teaching your children to be assertive, you are not only showing them how to openly and capably verbalize their feelings; you are also offering them a path that leads to self-empowerment.

Many books have been dedicated to teaching people how to be assertive. You are encouraged to examine such books if you feel the need to do so following your review of this strategy. However, for the most part, you are being assertive when you can directly state how you feel to another person according to three very simple sentences:

1. I feel_____when_____because_____.
2. What I need from you is _____.
3. Do you understand what I need from you?

In total, five bits of information are required to complete these assertive sentences:

1. I feel:
   A specific statement about how you feel—positive or negative.
2. When:
   A specific statement about the other person's behavior that caused you to feel positive or negative.

3. Because:

A specific statement about how the other person's behavior caused you to feel positive or negative.

4. What I need from you is:

A specific statement about what you need from the other person to improve the relationship and feel better.

5. Do you understand what I need from you?

A specific question to make sure the other person understands what you need to improve the relationship and feel better.

Notice how the process of being assertive focuses on the specific elements of feelings, behaviors, needs, and understanding. Let's address these elements one at a time.

Feelings relate to what is causing your positive or negative internal state: joy, anger, gladness, sadness, excitement, and many more such feelings. Behaviors are what you can observe another person doing that causes you to feel a specific way. Everyday examples might include some of the following positive and negative behaviors your son or daughter may exhibit that you can clearly observe:

- Your son prepares dinner for you (positive).
- Your daughter is reading while you are talking to her (negative).
- Your daughter tries to watch TV during Hopeful Hour (negative).
- Your daughter cleans the house for you when you are sick (positive).
- Your son ignores you while you are asking him a question (negative).
- Your son misses curfew two days in a row (negative).
- Your daughter takes out the trash without prompting (positive).

The main point here is to show how crucial it is to concentrate on what the other person is doing—observable behavior—rather than attempting to make statements about that person's internal processes. We can see behaviors (external processes); we cannot see what the other person is feeling or thinking (internal processes). That is why being assertive focuses on what we can actually perceive and witness. Let's take this a step further by practically applying this three-sentence approach to a couple examples of negative behaviors.

> *Child's behavior*: Reading the newspaper while you are talking.
> *Parent's assertive response*: "I feel ignored when you read the paper while I am talking to you because it makes me think that you don't want to listen to me.
>> What I need from you is to pay attention when I am talking to you.
>> Do you understand what I need from you?"

> *Teenager's behavior*: Misses curfew two days in a row.
> *Parent's assertive response*: "I feel mad and scared when you miss your curfew as you have done for the last two days. I feel this way because it shows me that you don't respect the rules we agreed to and that you don't take me seriously when I tell you that I worry about you when you are late.
>> What I need from you is to respect our house rules by being home on time, as we agreed, and to call immediately if there is something that may cause you to be late.
>> Do you understand what I need from you?"

This demonstration concentrated exclusively on negative behaviors, because most often when we need to be assertive, we are feeling upset based on what we perceive as negative behavior on the part of others. Take notice, however, that despite feeling upset, the parent does not become verbally aggressive. Aggressive forms of communication set out to verbally offend or attack the other person: "You idiot, put away that stupid paper and listen to me or else." Conversely, assertive communication is all about stating what a person sees, feels, and needs to feel better without hurting the other person. The focus is always on how the offended person feels as a result of the offending person's observable behavior. Assertiveness consistently addresses what the other person is doing (external behavior) rather than thinking or feeling (internal processes).

Referring once more to the previous examples, recognize how this assertive sequence makes a request of the child to exhibit more positive behavior. This relates to what the parent needs to improve the quality of the relationship and to feel better. This request is commonly prefaced with "What I need from you is ..." followed by a specific request for behavioral changes in the child. Once the needs are stated, this three-sentence assertiveness sequence ends with a question: "Do you understand what I need from you?" This question is intended to prompt the other person to restate and confirm what the requesting person needs to resolve the negative situation. Understanding is crucial to the assertive process; without it there can be no positive resolution. Asking this question is the easiest way to gauge a person's comprehension of and motivation to fulfill another's needs.

Many times this question of understanding will invite the other person to respond with feedback, particularly if there is a difference of opinion about how that person's behavior is being perceived. Feedback is welcomed because there is always another way of looking at the same situation. Regardless of the circumstances, we should all be afforded the opportunity to share our viewpoint since relationships are about relating. Therefore, both sides must be heard and understood before a mutually beneficial resolution can be achieved. Assertiveness mandates that a person be open to and highly conscious of the belief that there are always two sides to every story. This assertive process continues until there is agreement to manifest behaviors that resolve the presenting conflict.

Hopeful Hour Tip

Recap the basics of assertiveness from this chapter, focusing on feelings, behaviors, needs, and understanding. Give examples of the three-sentence formula for assertive response. Then give everyone scrap paper and pencils. Make up some fictitious situations, both positive and negative. Each person writes a one-line description of a behavior. This can be something that really happens in your household or something that is completely made up. Take turns role-playing how to use assertive, open communication in that situation.

Meet Jason and Nicki

To understand how to be open even when we are upset, let's apply the various strategies of this section to a tense situation between a father and his teenage daughter. Father and daughter have been working on open communication during Hopeful Hour times, and the hard work is about to pay off. Pay attention to how these strategies are woven into the presentation. Try to imagine how you would handle a similar situation between you and your child as you read how this father and daughter openly resolve their differences.

Here's the scenario: Jason is a single father of two children: Nicki, age fifteen, and Devin, age eight. Recently, Jason notices how Nicki is occasionally using profanity. On two separate occasions he directly asks her to stop using profane language. The first time Jason asks her to do this, she is walking her friend to the front door of the family home. When he makes the request, she responds in a curt tone, "Whatever!" The next day, Jason makes the same request after hearing her use similar words while talking on the phone. Following Jason's directive, Nicki covers the receiver of the phone and retorts in an agitated voice, "Can't you see I'm on the phone?" With that, she turns her back to him and continues her conversation.

While staring angrily at his daughter's back, Jason decides to Take Ten. Jason uses this strategy because he has learned from past experiences that when he is mad and reacts to his first impulse, tempers flare and little is ever accomplished; in fact, matters often got worse. Since adopting this time-out approach, Jason feels more in control, and the quality of his interactions with others, especially his kids, has gotten much better. In the past few weeks, his kids have also started using this approach when they get upset, even though they initially perceived it as "weird." In his own words, here is what Jason has taught his kids about their power to choose no matter what the situation:

Every action is a choice. So, no matter what the situation, you have the power to choose your response. No one can make you do anything you don't want to do. Remember: Think. Choose. Act.

During these ten-second breaks, Jason breathes deliberately and calmly while considering his next move. When he is mad, as he is in this situation, he has also learned to ask himself a very important question: "Do I feel in control?" If yes, he stays where he is and continues to consider his next move. If he does not feel in control, he says so and removes himself from the situation that is causing him to feel angry. At this time, Jason feels in control, so he stays put and continues considering his options. Here is what Jason thought about and decided to do during this time-out: I am tired, and tomorrow is going to be a hectic day. The last thing I need is to have this escalate into a heated argument. Part of me thinks this is a phase she is going through and I should ignore it, but another part of me realizes that if I don't say something soon, she will keep pushing the limits. It is best that I assertively deal with it tomorrow when things are not so uptight.

The next day, about an hour before dinner, Nicki returns from drama rehearsal, where she is preparing for an upcoming play. Looking content, she says, "Hello" and mentions that she is really starting to get her lines down. Jason praises her and tells her that he is looking forward to seeing her in the play. Nicki reminds him to be there on opening night.

Jason: I wouldn't miss it for the world.

Nicki: Cool *(Heads toward her room)*

Jason: Can you give me a few minutes? I'd like to go over something with you.

Nicki: Is it important?

Jason: *(looking at her firmly)* Yes, it is.

Nicki: Can I have a few minutes to get cleaned up?

Jason: No problem. Let's meet in the living room in fifteen minutes.

Minutes later, Jason offers Nicki a seat on the couch with him as she enters the living room. Prior to speaking he makes sure to uncross his legs because he knows how this type of body language may communicate something other than what he wants to say. Jason wants to be open verbally and physically. Moreover, he keeps the tenets of the three Rs of communication (Receive, Respect, Respond) in the forefront of his mind. Facing her, he sincerely thanks her for giving him some time out of her busy schedule to talk with him. While taking in a relaxing breath, he reminds himself to maintain eye contact and to be calm and direct. He begins in a concerned tone.

Jason: The last couple days have been tense between you and me. That is why I asked you to sit down with me tonight. I want to find a way for us to get along better. Let me get to the point: I feel upset and disrespected when you use cuss words like you did when your friend was over the other day and while you were on the phone last night because it shows me that you are not listening to me and that you are not taking this issue very seriously. What I need from you is to show me that you are respecting my requests and rules by using acceptable words to express what you are feeling rather than profanity. Do you understand what I am asking you to do?

Nicki: Dad, I know you are being assertive with me right now because you are using those words you taught me a few weeks ago.

Jason: Yes, I am being assertive, because I want to make sure you understand that how you speak to others, as well as to me, is very important to me. Now, do you know what I need you to do?

Nicki: Dad, I know what you are asking me to do, but I don't think you know how I feel. You always tell me there are two sides to every story, so I want you to hear my side. Okay?

Jason: All right, tell me what is on your mind.

Nicki: First, let me calm down for a second. I'm not mad or anything, just a little upset, but not mad. Do you know what I mean?

Jason: I know exactly what you mean because that is how I was feeling the other night when you were on the phone with your back to me. I actually had to take ten. Maybe you should do the same.

Nicki: That is probably a good idea. *(She takes in some deep breaths and looks down at the coffee table while thinking about what she will say and do next.)* Okay, here I go. Dad, I feel embarrassed and disrespected when you talk down to me in front of my friends, like when Shelly was over the other day and when I was talking to Lisa on the phone last night. I feel embarrassed and disrespected because it shows me that you think I am still a little girl. I'm not—I'll be sixteen pretty soon! What I need you to do is to talk to me like an adult and to be more aware of what you say to me around my friends. Do you understand what I need from you?

Jason: I am trying to understand you, but I had no idea that you felt this way. And for sure, I didn't know that you felt I was talking down to you and treating you like a little girl. Can you give me some examples of what I say so I can realize what I do that is causing you to feel this way?

Nicki: I can't remember them all right now, but I do recall the one incident you brought up earlier. Do you remember when you were talking about the time when Shelly was at our house a couple days ago?

Jason: Yeah, the girl with the weird hair.

Nicki: Her name is Shelly, and she has great hair. Anyway, when we were hangin' out in my room, you yelled out: "Keep it down girls—or go outside if you are going to be so loud!" Do you remember saying that?

Jason: For the most part. I think I was trying to get some work done. Are you sure I said that?

Nicki: Dad, trust me on this one; that is exactly what you said! I know, because felt so embarrassed when Shelly asked me, "Does your dad think we're in kindergarten or something?" I was cussing because Shelly wanted to leave after you yelled at us. She felt very uncomfortable, and I got really pissed-off! Oops—sorry—i didn't mean to say that. What I mean is, I was very angry when you told me to stop swearing right in front of Shelly as she was leaving. It only made the situation worse.

Jason: Sounds like we had quite a misunderstanding going on. Maybe I—

Nicki: Hold on. I have one more situation to tell you about. Do you remember when I was on the phone last night and I got mad?

Jason: Boy, do I ever! That was the one incident that got me worked up too, and it was the one that made me decide to sit down with you tonight.

Nicki: Good. Let me tell you my version: the whole time I was on the phone with my friend Lisa, you kept pointing to your watch and saying, "It's time for bed!" Lisa heard you a few times and laughed at me because her parents don't tell her when it's time to go to bed. Dad, all I wanted was for you to just leave me alone, but you kept doing that "It's-time-for-bed" thing every two minutes. It really got to me about the fifth time around. Do you know what I mean?

Jason: I think I'm starting to get it. Is there anything else?

Nicki: Yes, there is. Dad, I need you to respect my freedom and my space by letting me decide when it is time for bed rather than you telling me when it is time for bed.

Jason: I'll tell you what, since you are almost sixteen, I'll let you decide when you want to go to bed as long as you get up on time for school. And I will work on talking to you on a more mature, adult level. Are you okay with that?

Nicki: Exactly! I guess it's my turn now. Let me make sure I understand what you need from me. Basically, you want me to work on using, as you would say, "appropriate words" when I feel upset rather than profanity. I can't promise I won't blow it like I did a minute ago, but I will give it my best effort. Does that seem fair to you?

Jason: That seems fair to me. I feel like we are back on track now. And remember, you are on your own tonight when it comes to going to bed, so don't expect me to come tuck you in.

Nicki: Dad, you never stop. Anyway, thanks for understanding me by letting me choose my bedtime and agreeing to treat me more like an adult.

Jason: You're welcome.

Nicki: I'm really glad we had this talk. This assertiveness

thing really helps me to say what I feel when I am upset. I
got a lot off my chest.

Jason: Me, too. Now let's eat—I'm starved.

OPEN COMMUNICATION PAYS OFF

At the very minimum, openness will lead you to develop a deeper, more trusting and more loving relationship with each of your sons and daughters. This benefit alone is worth any discomfort you may experience initially while learning how to be open with your children.

As you show your kids that you are willing to openly talk about the hard, confusing issues they will inevitably face in their lives, they will be more willing to seek your input when difficult times strike and difficult decisions have to be made. Do this consistently and you will have earned the right to be the first person to influence them when they are worn down and extremely vulnerable. As a result, their decisions and subsequent actions will reflect your wisdom. Just as important, by teaching them how to openly and assertively communicate their feelings when they feel hurt, upset, or violated, you will have empowered them to resolve adverse and potentially dangerous situations when you can't be there. This lesson will last not just for today, but also for the rest of their lives. For this very reason, make the commitment to put these strategies to work in your family today. You will soon discover that there are no limits to the extraordinary benefits your family will experience over the course of a lifetime.

OPEN ASSIGNMENTS

OPEN Assignment 1: *Make a commitment to being open.*

Openness begins with a commitment to being open. With this essential first step in mind, commit or recommit yourself to being open with your children right now by going to www.hopefulkids.com and printing off and signing the Open Communication Certificate. This will demonstrate that you have made a lifetime commitment to practicing openness with yourself and your family. If there are two parents involved, both should sign. Remember, openness is a powerful process for developing a more trusting, meaningful, and loving relationship with your family.

I commit to open communication with my children.

_____

Parent's signature   Date

_____

Parent's signature   Date

OPEN Assignment 2: *Create an invitation for your children to be open with you.*

The next step in cultivating an open relationship with your children is to invite them to be open with you. To make this easier for you, this assignment is designed to help you create an invitation that you are comfortable in using with your kids. All you have to do is decide if you want to use the scripted examples from the previous strategies (see Strategies 1, 2, and 3) or create your own using these examples as a guide. Also, as a reminder, if you feel uncomfortable about doing this, admitting your fear is one of the best ways to begin being open with your children (see Strategy 3). Below, create your personal invitation for being open with your kids:

> ### My Invitation for Being Open with My Kids.
>
> _____
>
> _____
>
> _____
>
> _____
>
> _____

OPEN Assignment 3: *Invite your children to be open with you.*

Now that you have created an invitation you are comfortable to use, make the invitation as soon as possible. To fulfill this assignment, identify the actual day (date and time) you will sit down with your kid(s) to make the invitation, then follow through and do it. You can do this during a Hopeful Hour, or you might prefer doing it around the dinner table or some other family activity. Once you have done this, ask this follow-up question: "Do you feel okay about being open with me?" Don't worry about what will happen—just ask the question and see what happens.

> ### I Invited My Children To Be Open With Me.
>
> _____
> Parent's signature   Date

OPEN Assignment 4: *Find real-life examples.*

You learned in OPEN Strategy 8 that assertiveness is a highly effective method for expressing your feelings when you are upset. For the purposes of this assignment then, list two events in your recent past when you got upset following your observation of negative behavior from your kid(s). For example, you may list something like this: "When Billy came home three hours late from school without calling." List two real-life examples below:

Find Real Life Examples:

1. _____

2. _____

OPEN Assignment 5: *Apply the three-sentence formula to real examples.*

Using the three-sentence assertiveness method you learned in Strategy 8, apply it to the events you documented above by filling in the following blanks. Note: If you are still upset about any one of these events, use this as an opportunity to assertively communicate your feelings to the child who displayed the negative behavior.

Event 1:

I feel _____

_____

when _____

_____

because _____

_____.

What I need from you is _____

_____.

Do you understand what I need from you?

Event 2:

I feel _____

_____

when _____

_____

because _____

_____.

What I need from you is _____

_____.

Do you understand what I need from you?

HOPEFUL HOUR PLANNING PAGE

Write in your own words the main substance of Principle 2: OPEN

Plan how many Hopeful Hours you think you'll need to devote to this principle. List the dates you will have these Hopeful Hours. Jot down a key activity you will use in each Hopeful Hour to engage your children in learning the principle. Your activities may be suggestions you find in the chapter or adaptations you know your child will enjoy. Make sure your plan includes all the key strategies of the principle. Continue on an additional sheet of paper if necessary.

	Date	Strategy	Key Activity

CHAPTER 5

Principle 3: PURPOSE (Part 1)

OBJECTIVE 3a: Discovering your child's purpose.

Lance Armstrong, Ludwig van Beethoven, George W. Bush, Celine Dion, Billy Graham, Katherine Hepburn, Michael Jordan, Dr. Martin Luther King Jr., Abraham Lincoln, Nelson Mandela, Sandra Day O'Connor, Julia Roberts, William Shakespeare, Mother Teresa, Barbara Walters and Oprah Winfrey? What do all of these men and women have in common?

Answer: a clear sense of purpose! All of these famous individuals have made or are still making significant contributions to their fields and the world in general. They each attained phenomenal success because they believed they could create the life they wanted through their choices and goals. Stated plainly, purpose was their driving force, and this guided them to become hopeful.

Hope flows from purpose. Purpose is the foundation upon which hope is built. It gives focus and meaning to life. Purposeful people are hopeful people. Purpose is the one, clear factor that separates hopeful people from hopeless people. Purpose represents that vision of what we can be and what we can create through our choices and goals. In basic terms, *purpose* represents our *goals* while choices represent the actions we initiate to achieve our goals. Once a person masters this purposeful process of setting goals and choosing actions that support the attainment of those goals, personal power results.

As you recall, the primary mission of HOPEFUL is to show you how to develop your children into Hopeful Kids. Remember the seven principles?

H	HOUR
O	OPEN
P	PURPOSE
E	EXAMPLE
F	FIND
U	UNDERSTAND
L	LOVE

Hopeful Kids, and hopeful people in general, are defined and characterized by the Hopeful Motto: "I can create the life I want through positive choices and goals." This is the most direct and fundamental expression of individual purpose. Furthermore, taken as a whole, these twelve words embody what hopeful people believe and how they live. When young people can believe what this simple yet potent sentence represents, they will have discovered their capacity to create the life they want through their unique purpose. Ultimately, they will have become Hopeful Kids. And when this happens, they will have realized their personal power: personal power over their lives, personal power over peer pressure and personal power over hopelessness. For this reason alone, purpose is inseparable from the hopeful process. It is the catalyst that gives rise to hope, so it's essential to discover your child's purpose.

PURPOSE STRATEGIES (PART 1)

Purpose Strategy 1: *Teach your child the Hopeful Motto: "I can create the life I want through positive choices and goals."*

In truth, these are twelve of the most powerful words you can teach your child. They succinctly represent the qualities and attitude of a hopeful person. Accordingly, the Hopeful Motto will serve as our guide to discover your child's purpose so that he or she can become a Hopeful Kid. This section is specifically designed to help you achieve this end. As a refresher, let's review what the key terms of the Hopeful Motto mean in relation to Hopeful Kids:

"I can … create … the life I want …through positive choices and goals."

I can …
Hopeful Kids believe in their ability to create the life they want through positive choices and goals. These goals constitute their purpose.

create …
Hopeful Kids have the confidence and competence to set into motion purposeful action that will result in the life they desire.

the life I want …
Hopeful Kids define what they want to accomplish in life in the form of positive goals, then they initiate choices to achieve those goals.

through positive choices and goals.
Hopeful Kids are focused on positive choices and goals that will support

what they want out of life. They take responsibility for their actions by ensuring their choices are in line with their positive goals. This guides their behavior toward positive results.

This motto is the definition of a Hopeful Kid and the cornerstone of HOPEFUL for this basic reason: When your children believe it, they will become it! They will be Hopeful Kids. It is that simple. By introducing kids to this life-changing, hope-building motto as early as possible, you will be giving them a preview of what is to come while simultaneously planting the seeds that will eventually lead them to understand the significance of making positive choices and setting positive goals: The power to create the life they want.

Please be aware that when you first introduce children to this motto, they may feel a little confused. That is expected. But as you consistently and repetitively expose them to it, they will become more familiar with it and begin to truly understand what it has to offer them personally. Furthermore, as you guide kids to develop their purpose using the various strategies that follow, they will start to experiment and apply it to their lives. And each time they experience success in using it, they will come to believe: "I can create the life I want through positive choices and goals." When—not if—your kids reach this point, they will be ready to declare they are Hopeful Kids.

Here are some recommendations for teaching your kids the Hopeful Motto:

1. Go over the motto with them during your family's Hopeful Hour at least once a month.

2. Have them write it down in their own writing in big, bold letters in their Hopeful Kid's Notebooks or on a sign they will display in their rooms.

3. Ask them if they know what it means and have them explain it in their own words. Find some ways to personalize it for them in terms of the present and the future. For example, you might ask,

"How are you doing this right now?" and "How does what you do today effect what your life will be like in the future?"

4.   Have them repeat the motto out loud until they can say it from memory. You may want to make a game out of this if it helps.

5.   Post the Hopeful Motto where they will be reminded of it often.

6.   Finally, get them in the habit of saying the motto to themselves ten times in the morning and ten times in the evening before they go to bed.

It is important that you keep experimenting with this strategy until your child learns the Hopeful Motto, because it is the first step to becoming a Hopeful Kid and developing the life he or she wants. Think of the learning process this way: Familiarity leads to comfort; comfort leads to understanding; understanding leads to execution; execution leads to belief; belief leads to a way of life. In this case, it will lead to a purposeful way of life for you and your child.

The strategies that follow are designed to teach you how to systematically guide your children to believe in the Hopeful Motto, one purposeful step at a time. Keep in mind that what applies to your children also applies to you. Hence, teach and model these purpose-promoting strategies because, as you will learn in Principle 4: EXAMPLE, your kids will look to you to be an example of what you teach before they are willing to put it into practice. Remember, we teach most effectively through demonstration—actions over words. That said, teach by example by putting the Hopeful Motto into practice. Believe it and you will become it.

PURPOSE Strategy 2: *Remind yourself on a daily basis that your primary purpose is to help your child become a Hopeful Kid.*

You already know this because you would not be at this point in the book if you weren't purposely committed to teaching your child how to become a Hopeful Kid. Nevertheless, it is essential that you remind yourself every day that one of your true purposes in life is to do whatever it takes to empower your kids and save them from bad choices. By committing yourself and your children to HOPEFUL, you have resolutely declared you are up to the challenge. Now, write this goal down to keep you focused on your primary purpose: "I will do whatever it takes to help my child become a Hopeful Kid." Post it somewhere conspicuous where you will see it often. Allow the passion that is captured in these bold words to flow from you as you demonstrate purposeful action toward your kids. As you do this, also remind yourself daily that you are on your way to becoming a Hopeful Parent. Accelerate this transition by writing out the Hopeful Motto directly under your primary purpose: "I can create the life I want through positive choices and goals."

Take notice of how these two statements complement one another. By ensuring that your choices and actions are constantly reinforcing your primary purpose of helping your child become a Hopeful Kid, you are simultaneously creating the life you desire while becoming a Hopeful Parent. Armed with these two powerful declarations, nothing can stop you from realizing your purpose:

1.   I will do whatever it takes to help my child become a Hopeful Kid.
2.   I can create the life I want through positive choices and goals.

Repeat these purposeful goals out loud to yourself every morning and evening for the next thirty days. As you do this, your confidence and hope will begin to soar. Then, one glorious day it will happen; you will suddenly realize, "I can do this."

PURPOSE Strategy 3: *Use the P-5 Method to discover your child's Purpose.*

1. Positive 2. Passion 3. Purpose 4. Plan 5. Power
Developing a kid's purpose is not a complicated or arduous process.

Actually, it is quite straightforward and simple when you follow these steps based on the P-5 Method:

1.   Identify your child's positive traits.
2.   Create your child's passion profile.
3.   Discover your child's purpose.
4.   Develop your child's action plan.
5.   Unleash your child's personal power.

This is a cause-and-effect method. That is to say, each step builds upon, promotes and constantly interacts with the other steps. Thus, it is vital that you follow each of these steps in sequence, because in step 5, you will organize all this insightful information to develop your child's Hopeful Constitution. This mighty little document holds the key to unleash your kid's personal power.

HOPEFUL HOUR TIP

 The P-5 Method will take more than one Hopeful Hour. Don't rush the process. Even if you need to spend more than one hour on each step, that's okay. Go at the speed that allows your child to absorb the concepts. These activities are key to a long-term understanding of purpose.

Step P-1: Identify your child's POSITIVE traits

When children are aware of their strengths, they will be more prone to displaying them when they are challenged, thereby compelling them to remain focused on realizing their positive goals. Put a little differently, when something or someone tries to lure them away from their purpose, they will rely on their strengths to stay on track. Also, by gaining awareness of your children's positive traits, you will be better prepared to help them maintain purposeful momentum when challenges arise. Finally, by constantly reinforcing your kids' strengths, you'll keep them mindful of what they can do as opposed to what they cannot do.

The first thing you will need to do to accomplish this objective is to find one hour of undisturbed quiet time. Clear your mind of any distracting clutter and relax. In your spiral notebook, brainstorm what you think your child's positive traits and strengths are.

The first positive trait you will place on your list, no matter what, will be your child's ability to make positive choices. This is based on the premise that you get what you believe. In practical terms, if you believe your daughter can make positive choices that support her purpose, she will demonstrate a greater propensity to follow through with the expected behavior. Remember, behavior follows belief. Believe it; get it. Following this trait, write down each strength immediately as it pops into your mind. This could be anything related to humor, perseverance, intelligence, decision-making ability, a strong sense of right and wrong, assertiveness, imagination, creativity, a gift of gab, athletic talent, artistic ability— basically, anything and everything that is positive about your kid.

If you have more than one child, one hour should be sufficient for several kids.

Do this brainstorming exercise for fifteen minutes, or as long as it takes, and try to create a list of twenty or more positive traits. Next, group similar traits together by finding the most positive word or short phrase that best captures what you are trying to say. Once you have grouped the traits, narrow them down to what you feel are your kid's top ten positive traits. Remember, the first one on your list is your child's ability to make positive choices. Now, write each of these positive traits on a separate piece of paper. Hold on to this list because you will use it with your child in the next exercise. (Alternative: If it works best for your family, you can skip this step of completing the list on your own and complete your list along with your child in the next step of this strategy.)

All right, the second thing is to sit down with your children during Hopeful Hour and have them do exactly what you did earlier. Specifically, ask this question: "What do you think your positive traits and strengths are?" For a younger child, ask, "What do you think you are really good at doing?" Help kids to think about what they are trying to write down by pointing out your belief that making positive choices is one of their main strengths. Give some specific examples of how you have seen your kids do this. Beyond this hint, let kids brainstorm and write on their own. When they have completed the list (ten or more items), spend some time comparing and talking about the similarities and differences between your lists and their lists. Explain why you chose certain traits, particularly the ability to make positive choices. Now, encourage children to explain why they feel these traits describe what they do well. Once again, get them to talk about their capacity to make positive choices. Make sure to point out that you feel this is definitely their number one strength.

HOPEFUL HOUR TIP

If your child is too young or reluctant to write, you will have to be the writer for this strategy as well as other strategies and exercises that require writing. You could also ask a child to draw the activities he or she is good at.

After you have done this, ask kids to list their top five positive traits on a separate piece of paper titled, "My Positive Traits" in their Hopeful Kids Notebooks. Have them write using "I" statements. By now you should know which positive trait should appear first on the list.

Here are two examples created by Gina Myers, age fourteen, and Zack Richards, age twelve:

MY POSITIVE TRAITS BY GINA MYERS

1.   I know how to make positive choices.
2.   I am an excellent actress.
3.   I am good at math.
4.   I am very mature.
5.   I get along well with others.

MY POSITIVE TRAITS BY ZACK RICHARDS

1.   I know how to make positive choices.
2.   I am smart.
3.   I know how to help my family.
4.   I am a good basketball player.
5.   I can read well.

Have each child keep this list in a Hopeful Kids Notebook because you will use it later to compose the Hopeful Constitution. From this point forward, go out of your way to reinforce positive traits by praising kids with words and affection every time you see them exhibit positive behaviors, even ones that are not on the list. Let your children know how much you appreciate their positive attitude and how impressed you are with their ability to make positive choices that help create the life they want.

Step P-2: Create your child's PASSION profile
When you know the positive activities and desires your children are passionate about, you will know how to keep them motivated toward realizing goals or remotivating them when they are discouraged or off track. More important, passionate children are too busy doing what they enjoy to be duped into participating in the negative desires of others as a result of boredom and emptiness.

What is passion? Basically it can be defined as a strong urge to do or have something. A person's passion is primarily focused on activities and desires. Passion can take the form of work, a future goal, religion, a hobby, a volunteer activity, or anything else from which we gain enjoyment and feel strongly compelled to do or attain. With reference to purpose, passion is the bloodline that sustains purpose. It leads to and gives life to purpose. When we are passionate about something, we are committed to investing our energies and time to satisfying those compelling drives. We also tend to associate and surround ourselves with people who share similar interests. Put more directly, positive passions lead to positive peers. The opposite is also true: negative passions lead to negative peers.

Now how does passion relate to kids? Well, consider this for a moment. If you can assist your kids in realizing the positive activities and desires that turn them on, they won't feel pressured to be turned on by the negative causes of others. Bored and empty kids are victims waiting to volunteer. Equally important, they will be more apt to hang out with peers who share their favorable preferences and interests. Combine this with purpose and you have discovered how to empower your children to commit their time and energies to having a positive attitude, making positive choices, setting positive goals and developing positive friendships, and ultimately, a positive life. Positive begets positive.

Okay, let's get to work on creating your child's passion profile. For purposes of achieving our objective here, we will use the word passion to represent a kid's expression of what he or she enjoys doing most—positive activities—and what he or she wants to attain most. We will concentrate on positive activities and desires because they promote the development of hopeful behavior. The easiest way to determine your child's passion is to ask. That's right, with just a few short questions you will be able to find out, relatively quickly, what your kid enjoys doing most and what he or she most wants to attain. We will begin with positive activities.

Positive Activities: This represents the first half of the Passion Profile. To begin, sit down with your children during a Hopeful Hour and advise them that you want to use this time together to learn more about what makes them happy. Go on to say that beyond being fun, this will be very helpful to them because it will show them how to have a better, more positive life. Next, tell them that you are going to ask a few questions to find out what makes them happy. Make sure that they record their answers in a Hopeful Kids Notebook.

You will now ask one or both of these questions:

"What do you like to do more than anything else?"
"What activities make you the happiest?"

Instruct kids to write down everything that comes to mind. Clarify that you want them to list only those things they like doing the most—the things that make them the happiest. Do this for about ten to twenty minutes or however long it takes for each child to record a list. Then go over the list together. If you find activities that are inappropriate, spend some time explaining why you feel this way. Point out how these negative behaviors will cause, have caused, or are causing problems and unhappiness. Make it clear that these negative activities will not lead to a hopeful life but a hopeless life. Conversely, emphasize that positive activities will cause a child to have a better, happier life and ultimately to become a Hopeful Kid. Use the Hopeful Motto to explain your feelings by emphasizing the direct relationship between positive choices and goals with positive activities. Take whatever time you need to do this because it is important that your youngster understands the connection between negative activities and negative results. Remember, what we do directly affects what we get and how we feel. Positive actions lead to positive outcomes and feelings.

When this exercise is complete, have each child identify the top five positive activities that he or she enjoys doing the most. Again, have them explain to you why they enjoy doing these activities. Directly ask how these positive activities make them happy and how they help them get what they want from life and to become Hopeful Kids. Take this opportunity to really learn about what makes your kids tick. Finally, have them write down these activities using "I" statements on a separate piece of paper in the Hopeful Kids Notebook titled, "My Favorite Things to Do."

Here are some examples:

My Favorite Things to do by Gina Myers

1. I enjoy acting more than anything else.
2. I have the most fun in drama class.
3. I love watching old movies.
4. I like reading books about movie stars and acting.
5. I really like writing stories and poetry.

My Favorite Things to do by Zack Richards

1. I love learning about airplanes.
2. I love reading books about space travel.
3. I really enjoy working on car engines.
4. I like building stuff like go-carts and airplane models.
5. I love playing basketball.

Bear in mind that your child's list may be highly focused on one particular area (like the above lists) or it may be a list of five different activities. It doesn't matter. The most important thing is that it is a list of positive activities that your child enjoys doing most and that you and he are clearly aware of what those activities are.

Positive Desires: This represents the second half of the Passion Profile. Once again, you will employ inquiry as your primary strategy to guide your kids to define passion as it relates to positive desires. This will be accomplished through a process I refer to as Dreaming Out Loud. In essence, you will ask a series of questions designed to motivate children to openly and spontaneously think out loud about their deepest wants and wishes. Keep in mind that you are after the big picture here, so don't expect it all to make sense. We will bring order to this information later. For now, just go with the flow and have fun doing it. Do your best to foster honest expressions of desire and aspirations.

During a Hopeful Hour, relate to your children that you are very interested in learning more about what they want from life and what makes them happy. Have them get comfortable and give these instructions:

I am going to ask you some questions, then I want you to dream out loud. This means I want you to think and say whatever comes to mind. These questions will help you identify what you want most and what makes you most happy.

Convey that kids can dream out loud for as long as they want and that when they are done, you would like them to write down their top three desires. This segment will require you to ask four questions pertinent to future and present desires. These questions will assist your children in considering and deciding upon what they desire now and later in life. Also, just as you did previously, openly evaluate any responses that aren't supportive of the Hopeful Motto. If this is the case, work with your kid to identify positive desires. That said, see this as a prime opportunity to learn as much as you can about your kids' passion. We will transform these desires into achievable goals in the next step.

Ask each of the following four questions and encourage each child to dream out loud. Have kids write down each question, then record their top three desires on a page in the Hopeful Kids Notebook with this title: "What I Want Most from My Life." Feel free to modify these questions to fit your kid's particular needs and level of understanding.

FUTURE DESIRE QUESTIONS:

- What do you want most from your life in the future?
- How will these make you happy?

PRESENT DESIRE QUESTIONS:

- What do you want most from your life right now?
- How will these make you happy?

Here is what Gina and Zack created from this Dreaming Out Loud exercise:

What I Want Most from My Life by Gina Myers
What I want most from my life in the future:
- Be a famous actress.
- Win an Oscar.
- Live in a big city like New York or Los Angeles.

These will make me happy because:
- I will be in plays and movies.
- I can work with other actors and actresses.
- I will be able to live in a big city.

What I want most from my life right now:
- Get a part in my high school play.
- Go to an acting seminar.
- Go to a play in a big city.

These will make me happy because:
- I will have an opportunity to display my talents.
- The seminar will really help me prepare for my audition.
- By seeing a play I will get to see professionals perform.

What I Want Most from My Life by Zack Richards
What I want most from my life in the future:
- Be an airplane pilot.
- Graduate from the Air Force Academy.
- Build my own airplane.

These will make me happy because:
- I will be able to fly airplanes.

• I can travel and see the world.

• I will make good money.

What I want most from my life right now:

• Get better grades.

• Make the seventh grade basketball team.

• Get into Junior ROTC.

These will make me happy because:

• I will have the grades I will need to go to college.

• I will get to learn more about basketball.

• I will get a head start on learning about the Air Force.

When you have reached this point with your children, you will have learned what people, places and things excite and inspire them the most—their true passions. Together, these two lists, My Favorite Things to Do and What I Want Most from My Life, constitute your child's passion profile. The information contained in this profile is valuable because it offers a crystal-clear picture of what makes your child happy and a vision of the many opportunities that lie ahead. At the very moment of this realization, hope will take root. By coupling this with the next P, Purpose, you will show them how to achieve dreams one purposeful step at a time. Keep this passion profile handy because you will use it to produce your kid's Hopeful Constitution.

Step P-3: Discover your child's purpose

Children who know what their purpose is will have no time to get involved in activities or with peers that don't have similar goals. They will have a built-in radar system that can decipher good from bad, positive from negative, right from wrong. Consequently, their actions will center on fulfilling those positive goals that will help them get what they want from life today as well as the future.

So, what is purpose? Purpose is the translation of passion into achievable goals. It quantifies our expectations into action-focused behavior. It defines and demonstrates what we want most from life in the form of positive goals. Or, put simply, purpose is the conversion of our desires into deliverables. This is where we will create your son or daughter's purpose. And, as you recall, purpose encompasses a young person's goals, which translate into hope, an optimistic, confident outlook on life.

Hopeful Kids, therefore, are full of hope because they believe they have the power to create the life they want through positive choices and goals.

A youth's purpose can be considered his internal guidance system because it is where everything that competes for attention is scoped and evaluated. When opportunities favor their goals, kids will be compelled to pursue them. On the other hand, when situations contradict and interfere with accomplishing their goals, kids will be moved to disregard them. Children who lack purpose also lack this internal reference point to help them determine what will benefit or harm them. Additionally, because they lack a vision of what they can achieve and who they want to become, they are more likely to make bad choices and therefore are more prone to being victimized by corrupt people and destructive causes. They are literally gambling with their futures and lives because they are relying on chance to fill their void. This aimless approach depicts hopelessness and a life destined for failure and, eventually, destruction. Hence, by showing your child how to create and achieve positive goals, you will be filling that void with the confidence and skills he or she will need to devise a success plan for a lifetime. And that, folks, is the true definition of empowerment! Just as we did in the preceding steps, we will continue to ask some simple questions to develop those goals that will come to embody your son or daughter's purpose. Once again, within the context of a Hopeful Hour, prepare your kid for this new series of questions with this statement:

We have learned a lot about what makes you happy and what you really want out of life. Now it is time to create some goals to help you achieve what you want.

With that said, have your kids get out their passion profiles: "My Favorite Things to Do" and "What I Want Most from My Life." If it has been more than a few days since you helped your kids create the passion profile, spend some time getting reacquainted with all the positive activities and desires that your kids documented. While looking over the profiles, ask your kids if they would like to make any changes to either one of the lists. Let them think about the prospect of doing this on their own. If they choose to make some changes, have them update the list with new positive desires. Now your child is ready for a new set of questions.

To assist you in establishing your son or daughter's goals, we will use a technique I have labeled Working Backwards. This technique starts with the larger goal, then proceeds backwards until smaller, more manageable goals can be constructed. Try it exactly as it is laid out. Chances are great that it will produce this result: achievable goals. If for whatever reason this does not happen, experiment with it until that magical combination of questions and strategies emerges. Last, do your best to learn, have fun, and be creative with this purpose-focused process, because you will be repeating it many more times over the course of your child's hopeful development.

Begin by referring to the "What I Want Most from My Life" list. Pointing toward the desires listed under "What I want most from my life in the future," indicate that you want to help your child reach these big goals because you know how important they are. Refer to these goals as "big goals" because they embody large ideals and are well into the future. To illustrate this point, you may want to discuss how long your child thinks it will take to realize these larger objectives. You may even want to talk about some of the smaller goals to achieve before these bigger goals become a reality. This will help prepare a child mentally to identify and develop more immediate, achievable goals. Now, pointing to the desires your child listed under "What I want most from my life right now," go on to say that you will help your child achieve the big goals by concentrating on the goals that are most important right now.

It is worth explaining why we are starting with the present-day desires. They most accurately capture what is most relevant and meaningful to your child at this point, right now, today. Additionally, by teaching how to realize these more immediate desires, you will be showing how to realize the big goals as well. The goals a child sets right now may or may not be connected to life-goals the child establishes at a later age, but the experience is still powerful. Specifically, once kids master the basics of creating and realizing purpose, they will be ready to challenge themselves more and more until their most treasured dreams are within their grasp. The idea here is to start small to get big. Also, it doesn't matter where you start as long as you start somewhere positive. Somewhere positive is better than anywhere negative. It is the difference between being hopeful or hopeless.

Returning to the desires under "What I want most from my life right now," ask each child to identify which one of these desires is most important today. Guide them through this analysis by talking about priorities and timelines. Upon making a decision, have each child write it down in the Hopeful Kids Notebook. Here is what Gina and Zack selected:

> Gina: Go to an acting seminar.
> Zack: Get better grades.

With that decision, it is time to mold each of these desires into achievable goals. We will do this by getting some help from our expert consultant on goal setting: SAM (Specific, Achievable, and Measurable). Using Gina and Zack's choices, let's get SAM's advice.

Let's start with Gina: "Go to an acting seminar." According to SAM, Gina needs to be more specific about her goal. The easiest way to do this is to answer the five W's: Who, What, When, Where, and Why. Her parents already determined who (Gina) and why ("The seminar will really help me prepare for my audition.") earlier when they were helping her distinguish her desires. Applying the remaining three W's (What, When, Where) to Gina's goal, her parents asked her these questions:

Parents: What acting seminar?

Gina: It is called Teen Actors of America. It is really well known and it is recommended by my high school drama teacher.

Parents: When is the acting seminar?

Gina: It is scheduled during the last week of August: Thursday the 23rd through Saturday the 25th, 9 a.m. to 4:30 p.m. each day.

Parents: Where is the acting seminar?

Gina: The seminar will be conducted in the auditorium of my high school. On Saturday we will be going to a classic movie, but I'm not sure where yet. I will let you know as soon as I find out.

Once the specifics of her goal have been determined, Gina's parents then directed their questions to the last two letters of the SAM approach: Achievable and Measurable.

Parents: Gina, do you believe you can achieve this goal?

Gina: (in an enthusiastic tone) Oh yeah. Easily! I already have the prerequisites to get in. Plus, I have saved the $100 enrollment fee from my babysitting jobs. I can't wait to get started!

Realizing it was unnecessary to assist her in modifying her goal to make it more achievable, Gina's parents asked the next question regarding measurable:

Parents: What will you use to measure your success in completing this goal? In other words, how will you be able to tell you've achieved your goal?

Gina: Well, I'll actually go to the seminar every day. Then I will get a certificate of completion on the last day. Also, I will know I have accomplished what I want because I will have more knowledge about acting and be better prepared for my audition for the school play.

Satisfied with her answer, her parents worked with her to rewrite her goal so that it was more Specific, Achievable, and Measurable (SAM):

GINA'S GOAL

Goal #1: My goal is to successfully complete the Teen Actors of America seminar by August 25.

I will know I have achieved this goal when I receive a certificate of completion on the last day of the seminar.

Now it is time to work on Zack's goal: "Get better grades." Utilizing the same approach—SAM (Specific, Achievable, and Measurable)—Zack's parents began with questions to get Zack to be more specific by relying on the five W's: Who, What, When, Where, and Why. Since they previously established who (Zack), why ("I will have the grades I will need to go to college"), and where (school) they now proceeded to questions centered on determining what and when.

Parents: What do you mean by better grades?

Zack: I want to earn A's in all my classes from now on.

Parents: We admire your motivation to do well and we know you are smart, but do you think it is realistic to earn A's in every class for the next six years? I mean, don't you think you are setting yourself up for some disappointment? (Note: They are asking these types of questions to get Zack to consider how achievable his goal is.)

Zack: I never thought of it that way. Six years is a long time to get perfect grades in every class. (He thinks to himself for a moment.) Maybe I should shoot for A's and B's rather than just

straight A's. That is more realistic. But I will always do my best
to get an A.

Parents: That makes sense. How would you state your goal now?

Zack: My goal is to earn A's and B's in all my classes.

Parents: When do you see yourself accomplishing this goal?

Zack: Let's see (he takes some time to consider his options). To
get started, I will make this my goal for the first nine weeks of
school. That is when I will get my first report card.

Content with the specificity of his goal, Zack's parents concentrated
on the next two areas of SAM—achievable and measurable.

Parents: Zack, how achievable do you think your goal is now?

Zack: (*Zack reminds his parents of his past academic
accomplishments.*) I feel pretty good about being able to
achieve this goal.

Parents: Good. How will you know when you have achieved
your goal?

Zack: That's simple. I will get my report card in nine weeks
and it will tell me in black and white if I hit my bull's-eye.

Parents: Sounds like you know what you want. Now, let's
rewrite it so that it is specific, achievable, and measurable
(SAM).

After some thinking and additional dialogue with his parents,
Zack writes the following purpose-focused statement. Notice that he
states it in the form of a bull's-eye. (Note: We will discuss this strategy
very soon under "Reinforcing Your Child's Purpose"):

ZACK'S BULL'S-EYE

Bull's-eye #1: My bull's-eye is to earn A's and B's during the first
nine weeks of school.

I will know if I have hit my bull's-eye when I receive my November report card.

Pretty simple. Okay, at this juncture it is time to put a plan into place to achieve your child's objective. Please understand that we selected only one goal at this point because your kid is just learning how to establish and achieve purpose. The idea here is to create every opportunity possible for success, small to big. In recognition of this logic, it is best to start with a simple goal that can be achieved within thirty to ninety days. For younger children, ten and under, you may want to develop shorter-term goals that can be achieved within seven to fourteen days. As kids become more proficient with this process, you will encourage them to challenge themselves by setting more goals and broadening their purpose.

So don't fret if goals seem trivial; the process is important, and every success brings important lessons. Goals may be as simple as "Have a sleepover for my tenth birthday" or "Get an Xbox" or "Make first chair in the band" or "Collect cans of food for needy families." Whatever the goal, the process is the same: identify specific, achievable, measurable steps that will lead to accomplishing the larger goal.

The number of goals your child is pursuing at any one time depends on motivation to achieve. Motivation to achieve will increase in direct proportion to the incremental successes a child experiences while realizing goals. That is why you want to create as many opportunities for success as you can for your child during these formative weeks. In general, though, children six to ten years of age should be actively pursuing two to three main goals at any given time following three months of learning successful goal achievement. Kids who are eleven and older should be able to handle three to five goals once they have the basic process down. For now though, we will stick with this one goal and create every chance possible over the next four to twelve weeks for your child to succeed at realizing his goal. Remember: start small to get big.

AT MY HOUSE

 Look for opportunities to check in with your child's progress in encouraging ways. You don't have to wait for Hopeful Hour. You can ask a casual, friendly question on the way to the grocery store or at bedtime or whenever you have a quiet moment with your child. Be sure always to say something that expresses how much you believe in your child.

Step P-4: Develop your child's action plan

If you don't have a plan to succeed, you have a plan to fail. When your child plans time around purpose (positive goals), he or she will have little time to get sucked into the destructive plans of hopeless others. Ultimately, your child has a plan for becoming hopeful.

A plan is a schedule of activity organized toward achievement. It specifies how your kid will go about achieving the goal step by step, day by day. The easiest and most effective way to do this is based on two techniques you learned recently: Working Backwards and the five Ws (Who, What, When, Where and Why). Specifically, you would start with the larger goal, and then work backwards to develop smaller goals by asking questions based on the five W's:

Who: Determine who will have to be involved and their responsibilities: parents, friends, teachers, coaches, etc.

What: Determine what smaller activities or goals will have to be completed before the larger goal can be achieved: homework, practice, registration, preparation, assignments, etc.

When: Determine when these goal-centered activities will need to be conducted in the form of a schedule: specific dates and times.

Where: Determine where these smaller activities will need to be conducted: home, school, church, gymnasium, sports field, library, etc.

Why: Note: Use *why* questions only if your child is choosing a particular person, place or activity that does not seem to support accomplishing a goal. Your objective here is to get the child to independently evaluate and understand why a choice is not supportive of a goal. To do this, ask this question: "Do you understand why this (person, place or activity) will not help you achieve your goal?" Then, have your child explain to you why this is so. Should this be the case, work with the child to make more positive choices that will guide to success. Make sure he or she understands that the quality of choices now will determine the quality of outcomes later —good or bad.

Gina's and Zack's parents applied this approach to their children's goals. Here is the resulting "Plan" as it would appear with the respective goal or bull's-eye.

GINA'S GOAL

Goal #1: My goal is to complete the Teen Actors of America seminar by August 25th.

I will know I have achieved this goal when I receive a certificate of completion on the last day of the seminar.

Plan: I will register for my seminar on Friday, August 17th. I will attend the seminar August 23rd through August 25th, 9 a.m. to 4:30 p.m. each day in my high school auditorium. On August 25th, I will go to the movies with my class at the Hunt Theatre, 2 p.m. to 4 p.m.

ZACK'S BULL'S-EYE

Bull's Eye #1: My bull's-eye is to earn A's and B's during the first nine weeks of school.

I will know if I have hit my bull's-eye when I receive my November report card.

Plan: I will study Monday through Friday at home from 3 p.m. to 5 p.m. If I need to, I will study on Saturdays from 2 p.m. to 4 p.m. I will ask for help from my parents if I need it. If they can't help me, I will go to my teachers.

We're almost done. All we need to do now is to organize this insightful information to develop your kid's Hopeful Constitution. You will do this in the next and final step of this purposeful adventure. First, you are to be congratulated—outstanding! It has been a lot of work to get here. You can be assured the payoff will be worth the effort. All right, one more step.

HOPEFUL HOUR TIP

 You might choose to continue learning more Hopeful Strategies at the same time as you watch children achieve their first goals. Consider using a few minutes of each Hopeful Hour to remind them of key principles for achieving purpose before moving on to new material.

Step P-5: Unleash your child's personal power

Where a young person's knowledge of positive traits, passion, purpose and plans converge, personal power emerges. Personal power is actualized when a person realizes he or she can use this self-knowledge to create the life he or she wants through choices. Every positive choice to fulfill positive goals makes an individual that much more invested in fulfilling them. With this vested interest, a child will be less inclined to choose events or people that will reduce the value of purposeful investment. Positive choices are the most powerful investment strategy for creating the life we want. Remember: Choice is personal power in action.

In this last step of P-5, you will aid your child in organizing all of the self-knowledge he or she has gained from these various exercises to compose a Hopeful Constitution. Compared to the U.S. Constitution, here are a couple of compelling reasons why this mighty little document is so important to your child's hopeful development. First, just as the U.S. Constitution defines and declares what the United States is, the Hopeful Constitution defines and declares who your child is—what makes him happy, what he wants, and what he is capable of doing and becoming. Second, just as the U.S. Constitution guarantees each of us the right and the freedom to pursue our dreams, the Hopeful Constitution empowers your child with the ability and freedom to make his dreams come true. In short, the Hopeful Constitution is the key to unleashing your child's personal power because it is his personal blueprint for becoming a Hopeful Kid who believes, "I can create the life I want through my positive choices and goals."

To create your child's Hopeful Constitution, gather up all the information you have developed together in P-1 through P-4 in this order:

1. Hopeful Motto
2. Goal or Bull's-eye
3. My Positive Traits
4. My Favorite Things to Do
5. What I Want Most from My Life

You may want to complete the Hopeful Constitution on a computer with a word-processing program. This is because it will be easier to update your child's Hopeful Constitution as he or she accomplishes goals or desires change. If you don't own a computer, try to get access to one through a library, a school, or a friend. If for whatever reason this is not possible, no big deal; you will just have to do it the old-fashioned way:

pencil and paper. Next, have your child place this title at the very top and center of the page: "My Hopeful Constitution by (Your Child's Name)." Immediately following the title, transfer the information you gathered above onto this new piece of paper in this specific order: 1. Hopeful Motto; 2. Goal or Bull's-Eye; 3. My Positive Traits; 4. My Favorite Things to Do; and, 5. What I Want Most from My Life. When it is finished, it should resemble Gina and Zack's Hopeful Constitution:

MY HOPEFUL CONSTITUTION BY GINA MYERS

My Hopeful Motto: I can create the life I want through positive choices and goals.

> My Goals:
>
> Goal #1: My goal is to complete the Teen Actors of America seminar by August 25th.
>
> I will know I have achieved this goal when I receive a certificate of completion on the last day of the seminar.
>
> Plan: I will register for my seminar on Friday August 17th. I will attend the seminar August 23rd through August 25th, 9 a.m. to 4:30 p.m. each day in my high school auditorium. On August 25th, I will go to the movies with my class at the Hunt Theatre, 2 p.m. to 4 p.m.
>
> *Depending on the child, more goals might follow.*

My Positive Traits:

> 1. I know how to make positive choices.
> 2. I am an excellent actress.
> 3. I am good at math.
> 4. I am very mature.
> 5. I get along well with others.

My Favorite Things to Do:

> 1. I enjoy acting more than anything else.

2. I have the most fun in drama class.

3. I love watching old movies.

4. I like reading books about movie stars and acting.

5. I really like writing stories and poetry.

What I Want Most from My Life:

What I want most from my life in the future:
- Be a famous actress.
- Win an Oscar.
- Live in a big city like New York or Los Angeles.

These will make me happy because:
- I will be in plays and movies.
- I can work with other actors and actresses.
- I will be able to live in a big city.

What I want most from my life right now:
- Get a part in my high school play.
- Go to an acting seminar.
- Go to a play in a big city.

These will make me happy because:
- I will have an opportunity to display my talents.
- The seminar will really help me prepare for my audition.
- By seeing a play I will get to see professionals perform.

Now, let's take a look at Zack's Hopeful Constitution:

MY HOPEFUL CONSTITUTION BY ZACK RICHARDS

My Hopeful Motto: I can create the life I want through positive choices and goals.

My Bull's-Eyes:

Bull's-Eye #1: My bull's-eye is to earn A's and B's during the first nine weeks of school. I will know if I have hit my bull's-eye when I receive my November report card.

Plan: I will study Monday through Friday at home from 3 p.m. to 5 p.m. If I need to, I will study on Saturdays from 2 to 4 p.m. I will ask for help from my parents if I need it. If they can't help me, I will go to my teachers.

Depending on the child, more goals might follow.

My Strengths:

1. I know how to make positive choices.
2. I am smart.
3. I know how to help my family.
4. I am a good basketball player.
5. I can read well.

My Favorite Things to Do:

1. I love learning about airplanes.
2. I love reading books about space travel.
3. I really enjoy working on car engines.
4. I like building stuff like go-carts and airplane models.
5. I love playing basketball.

What I Want Most from My Life:

What I want most from my life in the future:

- Be an airplane pilot.
- Graduate from the Air Force Academy.
- Build my own airplane.

These will make me happy because:

- I will be able to fly airplanes.
- I can travel and see the world.
- I will make good money.

What I want most from my life right now:

- Get better grades.
- Make the seventh grade basketball team.
- Get into Junior ROTC.

These will make me happy because:
- I will have the grades I will need to go to college.
- I will get to learn more about basketball.
- I will get a head start on learning about the Air Force.

Awesome! You have just helped your child compose one of the most important literary works of his or her life. More important, however, your child created it, and only she can choose to change it. Now that's real power: The power to create the life she wants through choices! Best of all, you have just taught your kid the recipe for living a purposeful and hopeful life. Your child now knows who she is, what her strengths are, what she enjoys doing most, what her dreams are, what she wants to accomplish, when she wants to accomplish it, where she wants to make it happen, why she wants it, and how to make it happen. Wow—all of this on a couple pieces of paper. Small package, big results!

Gina and Zack seem to have a long-term perspective, and we'll visit them again later to see what happened with the goals that began in a Hopeful Constitution. Many kids will need consistent practice and coaching at setting and accomplishing goals before the long-term picture emerges. Don't worry if this takes a while; the Hopeful Constitution is meant to be a changing document that grows and matures with the child.

I strongly recommend that you review your child's Hopeful Constitution on a regular basis, perhaps once a month, and especially when he accomplishes a goal, because that means it's time to develop a new goal. Get in the habit of using P-5 to keep the Hopeful Constitution fresh and meaningful. Once it is developed, it will be a cinch to update. This will keep you in touch with what is going on in your child's life while keeping him focused on and in the habit of achieving goals. This last point can't be emphasized enough. The very core of HOPEFUL is creating your child's purpose. With it, there are no limits to the success and happiness your child will experience. Without it, your child is on the fast track to hopelessness and the aimless, empty life that follows. Purpose is the cure for hopelessness. Developing your kids' purpose is the surest way to keep them on a positive path, involved with positive peers, focused on positive goals, and most important—hopeful!

PURPOSE ASSIGNMENTS (Part 1)

PURPOSE Assignment 1: *Set your own goals.*

Use the P-5 Method to establish a few specific, achievable and measurable goals for yourself. If you use the method for yourself, you'll have more credibility in teaching it to your kids. You'll be able to see from personal experience where the pitfalls might be and plan how to help your kids navigate past them.

PURPOSE Assignment 2: *Complete the positive traits assignments.*

Set aside undistracted time to complete the exercise on identifying positive traits in your children. While you can do this together with your kids, some prior thinking will ensure you have something positive and encouraging to say if your kids get stuck in the process.

PURPOSE Assignment 3: *After thirty days, measure your own purpose.*

Refer back to the goals you set in Assignment 1. After thirty days, assess your own progress. Hold yourself accountable to the system you are teaching your children.

CHAPTER 6

Principle 3: PURPOSE (Part 2)

OBJECTIVE 3b: Reinforcing your child's purpose.

The power of choice. That's really what PURPOSE is all about. With our choices we create our lives. So why not use our choices to create the life we want? The previous chapter helped you to know how to lead your child through the process of discovering purpose. At the end of that process, your child should have a written document with some specific goals and plans for achieving those goals. Obviously, though, that is not the end of the process. Kids lose focus. Papers get lost. Good intentions disappear into the rush of everyday life.

Keep up your Hopeful Hour sessions with your family and keep the goals in front of your kids. In addition, look for other moments during the week when you can say something encouraging or ask a touch-base question to reinforce a child's purpose. This ongoing phase of reinforcement is just as important as the initial stage of discovering purpose. Reinforcing purpose keeps kids focused, motivated and responsible.

PURPOSE STRATEGIES (Part 2)

Purpose Strategy 4: *Teach your child the power of choice.*

In the United States, each of us is guaranteed the freedom to create the life we want through our choices—the pursuit of happiness. In fact, the very nature of freedom is manifested in our power to choose. This ultimately determines the life we live: good or bad, right or wrong, happy or sad, positive or negative. It is simply a matter of choice. Respecting this awesome potential, prove to your children that they have within them the unlimited ability to design, mold, and actualize the very lives they dream about through choices. Here are some ways to help kids appreciate and put into action the power of choice:

1. Use the Hopeful Constitution to show in black and white how making choices creates positive goals. Remind kids they are in complete control of the Hopeful Constitution, and only they can choose to change it.

2. Take every opportunity to reinforce the capacity to make positive choices and other positive traits and strengths.

3. Keep the Hopeful Motto in front of the whole family: "I can create the life I want through positive choices and goals."

4. Demonstrate the power of cause-and-effect: The choices we make today will impact the life we live tomorrow. Positive choices will result in positive outcomes and negative choices will result in negative outcomes. Let kids see you making positive choices that result in positive outcomes.

5.   Reinforce the value of this cause-and-effect reality by reminding kids that every action is a choice, even in times of emotional upset. Model Take Ten and Think–Choose–Act (see Principle 2: Open Strategy 6) and gently remind kids to use these tools themselves.

6.   When kids make choices that are in-sync with goals, reward them. Conversely, when they make choices that are out of sync with goals, respectfully show how the choice resulted in the negative outcome (cause-and-effect). This will help kids to be more conscious of their choices and more responsible for the results of those choices.

7.   In cases where choices are off-target, work to re-trace, re-think and re-try until a child develops an action plan that is on-target with the goal or bull's-eye. Role-play to make sure the child is prepared to follow through with the plan by anticipating the possible outcomes of behavior before acting.

You can see that none of these ideas are one-time actions. Use and reuse these tactics until your child believes he or she has the capacity and confidence—power—to make the choices that will accomplish goals and fulfill purpose. Remember, choice is the most powerful tool to build the life we want.

Purpose Strategy 5: *Create many mini-opportunities for success.*

Your child will become more comfortable and competent in pursuing larger, more sophisticated goals once she has experienced success in achieving smaller goals. This goes back to the philosophy of starting small to get big. Based on this logic, it is in the best interest of your child for you to create many small opportunities for success so that she can develop the desire and confidence to pursue bigger goals down the road. Of course, the term small is a relative term, because what one kid may consider small, another kid may consider gigantic. When this is the case, it is most often due to differences in age, maturity, and level of goal-achievement experience.

Your objective here is to identify a variety of goals that your child can easily accomplish until confidence reaches a level where your son or daughter is ready to develop and pursue more challenging goals.

Since it is impossible to create a list of opportunities that will fit the needs of every kid in every situation, you will have to use your knowledge of your child to create an effective list. The first thing is to identify a variety of positive activities that can be converted into goals. The best place to start would be your child's Hopeful Constitution. Go to the sections titled "My Positive Traits" and "My Favorite Things to Do." Now determine how you can translate some of these positive traits and activities into achievable, short-term goals with matching rewards. Don't forget to provide a little incentive to give something to look forward to as a child strives to reach the goal line. What follows is a list of potential ideas based on Gina and Zack's interests:

- Be able to tell me when you have made three positive choices this week, and I will make your favorite dinner.
- Present a small play for our family on Saturday night on anything you want and I will take you to a movie of your choice on Sunday.
- Show me you have read any book you want about airplanes, and I will take you out for ice cream.
- Write me a poem and I will frame it and hang it up.
- Draw me a picture of an airplane and I will frame it and hang it up.

Obviously, there are an infinite number of possibilities here. The key is to find those things that give your child passion and pride, then convert them into goals that have success written all over them. If your child is young or has just started to learn how to establish and achieve goals, start small. If, on the other hand, you child is somewhat familiar with doing this, take it up a notch and go from there.

AT MY HOUSE

Review each child's Hopeful Constitution. In your spiral notebook, brainstorm some small goals for each child in your family. In your next Hopeful Hour, present the goals, along with the reward you are offering for accomplishing each goal.

Once your child seems to have gotten comfortable accomplishing these smaller goals, transfer the role of establishing these goals to the child. Review the P-5 Method in PURPOSE Strategy 3 (chapter five). Whatever you do, continue to review your child's progress toward achieving goals on a regular basis—at least once a month—and develop new goals to take the place of the ones a child has accomplished. No matter what, though, do not allow your child to be without purpose, because a lack of vision and boredom invites trouble and hopelessness. As you recall, hopeless kids are victims waiting to volunteer.

HOPEFUL HOUR TIP

Younger children might enjoy a chart that visually reminds them of what they have accomplished. Gather some simple art supplies such as poster board and markers or paint. During a Hopeful Hour, work together to create a visual reminder of goals and a method to indicate when a child has accomplished one.

PURPOSE Strategy 6: *Schedule purposeful experiences.*

The idea here is to keep your child focused and motivated by scheduling activities that reinforce purpose. This demonstrates that you believe in what the child is doing because you are willing to take the time to find opportunities that support achieving the goal. Kids will appreciate the effort and become that much more excited about reaching goals. The easiest way to fulfill this strategy is to identify a variety of activities that your child wants to do as a result of purpose. During Hopeful Hour, ask kids to make a list of everything they would like to do that would help them learn more about those things that interest them most, as documented in the Hopeful Constitution. (At times, you may even want to do this on your own and surprise kids with a purposeful experience as a way of rewarding them for being positive and staying on-target.) Go through the list to ensure activities are aimed toward fulfilling purpose. Then schedule some time to do some of the things listed. Kids will look forward to these purposeful experiences with great anticipation since they will be able to see their purpose in action and spend time with you. Some examples of purposeful experiences based on Gina and Zack's lists might include:

- A professional or college basketball game on TV, complemented by some pizza.
- A trip to the local college to see a play.
- A trip to the local airport to look at and identify types of airplanes.
- A classical movie at home along with some homemade popcorn.
- An afternoon building a model airplane together.
- A trip to the local bookstore for a poetry reading.

You are limited only by your own imagination. Be creative and discover those experiences that excite and inspire your children the most. And each time you experience these purposeful moments together, marvel at the wonder in their eyes as they see themselves realizing their dreams. At that very instant, know that you have just witnessed something truly remarkable while moving your kids just that much closer to making it all come true.

PURPOSE Strategy 7: *Reinforce the positive: Believe it—get it!*

You know that behavior follows belief. Put this strategy to work to strengthen your children's ability to make positive choices and engage in positive activities.

Even if your kids do not believe in themselves at this moment, you must remain eternally optimistic that they will be able to make the right decision when the situation demands it. The more they see you believing in them, the more they will start to believe in themselves and, consequently, the more likely they will be to display the desired behavior. Boost self-confidence by reminding kids that you believe that their number one positive trait is the ability to make positive choices. Give this credence by pointing out when you have seen them make good choices. You may even want to turn this into a small goal and an opportunity for success by having kids keep track of how many positive choices they make over the course of a week. Then review these proof-positive examples during your Hopeful Hours. Also, make a deliberate effort to catch kids making good choices. And always, always, teach and model the art of making choices that are positively targeted toward purpose.

You can also use this same strategy to get kids back on track when they display negative behavior or get involved in negative activities. For instance, when they exhibit negative behavior, assertively tell them how it is affecting you and how you believe they are capable of being more positive based on their strengths. Give some examples. Furthermore, in those situations when you observe kids engaging in negative activities, get them refocused and recommitted to positive ventures by revisiting their Hopeful Constitutions. Point out how you thought that they enjoyed doing these positive activities more than anything else. Make sure to openly discuss the unfavorable consequences that will result from their continued involvement in negative activities and being pulled away from goals (cause and effect). Strengthen the power to choose by asking kids if they need to revise the Hopeful Constitution to create some other positive activities that are more in line with what they want out of life. Get kids to recommit to being positive in terms of choices, activities and peers by developing a viable action plan. Once again state your belief in kids' competence to make positive choices aimed at getting what they want out of life. Better yet, reinforce it with these heartfelt words: "I believe in you" often and see how this motivates them to make positive choices. Do this consistently, and eventually kids will believe in their own power to make it happen!

Now, let's learn how to reward your child for making it happen.

PURPOSE Strategy 8: *Reward the behavior you want.*

This strategy is similar to Strategy 6 in that it focuses on rewards for positive choices. However, rather than rewarding smaller actions that demonstrate good choices, plan to reward behaviors that keep kids focused on the goals they set in the Hopeful Constitution. Recognize the actions that incrementally move the child closer to achieving a goal and deliberately reward choices that support the achievement of positive goals. To start, you will need to make a list of all the possible rewards that will encourage your child to continue his purposeful momentum. This should be pretty easy since most parents know what their kid enjoys: pizza, ice cream, movies, pool parties, video games, a favorite meal, TV, arcades, theme parks, the circus, water parks, museums, concerts, a particular sport, go carts, camping, clothing, and the list goes on and on from here. If you need some ideas, ask your kids; they will be more than willing to help you out. Note: Praise, encouragement, recognition, and compliments are also very effective rewards. Sometimes something said is more meaningful than something given.

Once you have identified as many potential rewards as you can, prioritize them from the smallest to the biggest. For example: ice cream, favorite meal, movie, model airplane, new pair of sneakers, new outfit, new bike, concert tickets, and so on. Now decide which items you will use to reward positive actions toward attaining the goal versus achievement of the goal. Work with your child to specify what he or she will receive for trying to achieve the goal (action) and what he or she will receive for accomplishing the goal (achievement). Warning: Don't go overboard to get results; a little goes a long way. The idea here is to give your child something to look forward to for staying on-target and for achieving purposeful results. Whatever you do, though, reward positive behaviors only. Doing otherwise will give your child a mixed message about what is expected. You get what you reward. Hence, be very careful about what you reward because, whatever you reward will most likely happen again—positive or negative. Reward the positive and correct the negative.

PURPOSE Strategy 9: *No failure; only feedback.*

As your kids pursue goals, sometimes they will become discouraged with performance, frustrated by events beyond their control, or disappointed if they miss the mark. During these challenging times, the first thing you want to say is this: "You did not fail." This is because failure happens only when a child makes no effort to achieve positive goals. A child who was in the act of trying when he or she experienced the disappointment is still successful because he or she learned something from the experience. Teach that there is no failure, only feedback. As a definition, feedback is the lesson we learn from our mistakes. Mistakes are our best teachers. This is because they teach us how to do better the next time around.

HOPEFUL HOUR TIP

 Talk about "no failure, only feedback" in a neutral time, such as during Hopeful Hour. Introduce four instructional questions to ask when kids feel dejected or miss the mark.

1. What did you learn from this experience?
2. What could you have done differently?
3. What will you do the next time?
4. What is your plan to make this happen?

Then, when someone in the family experiences disappointment, bring up these questions to discuss in relation to the disappointment—and return to optimism. Use these questions to inspire kids to get back in the saddle and give it another try.

In cases of repeated discouragement, consider asking your child to modify the goal to make it more achievable and desirable. Work with the child to develop another goal that ignites enthusiasm again. Keep kids motivated by refreshing their memory that as long as they are trying, they are succeeding, and a mistake is just feedback indicating that they need to do something differently to get what they want. Teach kids to say to themselves, "As long as I am trying, I am succeeding." Eventually, you want kids to learn how to independently evaluate their own setbacks and mistakes. When they are able to do this, they will be well on their way to being in control of their choices.

The next strategy will show you in greater detail how to teach your child to independently evaluate options.

PURPOSE Strategy 10: *Strengthen your child's ability to make purposeful and responsible choices through independent evaluation.*

Independent evaluation, without a doubt, is one of the most important skills you can teach children. It is vital that kids learn how to independently evaluate their options before choosing a particular course of action. If they know how to do this, they will be more responsible for their actions and be more prone to stay focused on and committed to positive goals. And as you were shown previously, a Hopeful Kid is responsible for the outcomes of his or her choices—good or bad. A Hopeful Kid is a responsible kid.

The skill of independent evaluation cannot be developed within your child unless he or she has something against which to evaluate the options. That something is purpose. This is the internal reference point by which all options are evaluated. This is why it is so important that you work with your child to develop purpose—positive goals. A child with an intact sense of purpose is able to skillfully evaluate people and activities that are competing for attention and resources. The stronger the commitment to purpose, the more inclined a child will be to choose options that fit within the positive desires while avoiding contradictory or hazardous options. A child without purpose is willing to let someone or something else fill the void and give direction and meaning. Too often, this results in victimization and exploitation. Purpose, therefore, is the key to giving your child the proficiency to decipher the good from the bad and stay on target.

You can easily teach your child how to independently evaluate by constantly asking two simple questions when presented with options: "Will this help me achieve my goals?" or "Will this help me get what I want out of life?" Kids have two choices: Yes or No. If the answer is yes—based on evaluation that the presenting option will help achieve goals or help get what the child wants out of life, then the child can go for it! If, however, the answer is no, advise that he or she would be wise to find another option that is more supportive of positive desires. Strengthen this lesson by constantly reminding your child of this cause-and-effect reality: If you choose the behavior, you choose the outcome—good or bad. It's your choice.

HOPEFUL HOUR TIP

 You can better prepare your child for making positive choices by creating scenarios that realistically duplicate the challenges of real life. Brainstorm a list of situations that might happen in your child's life right now or in the next few years of development. Ask what kids would do in these situations and why. In more difficult situations, role-play to give a better sense of what to say and do to make the right choice. When kids are on-target, reinforce the ability to make positive choices. When they are off-target, work to develop an internal script—what kids can say to themselves—that results in an on-target choice.

Keep kids constantly aware of and accountable for the outcomes of their choices. Do this by respectfully reminding them that they, and only they, can make the choice that will result in a negative or positive outcome—cause and effect. In addition, remember to consistently reward responsibility and always work to correct negative, irresponsible behaviors. Independent evaluation leads to individual responsibility. Teach how to independently evaluate and you have taught kids how to make responsible, positive choices today—and for the rest of their lives.

The next strategy will show you a unique method for keeping your child on target.

PURPOSE Strategy 11: *BULL'S-EYE—a unique approach for keeping your child on target with purpose.*

The bull's-eye approach is highly effective in getting a child to focus on goals, evaluate options, and be more responsible. This is how it works:

Imagine each of your child's goals as individual bull's-eyes and the child's choices as individual arrows. Each goal is a bull's-eye because that is what the child is aiming to hit, and the choices are arrows because that is how the child is going to eventually hit the bull's-eye (achieve the goal). Get the picture?

To implement this strategy, make or buy targets with a distinct bull's-eye. (Paper plates work well as homemade targets.) Next, assist kids in writing each of their goals in the bull's-eye of a target. The number of goals should equal the number targets, i.e., three goals on three targets. Make sure that each goal is easy to read in the middle of the target. Hang it in a place where the child will see it frequently. Now constantly remind him or her to aim to strike the bull's-eye (goal) with each arrow (choices). Strengthen confidence by constantly reminding kids of their ability to make positive choices (arrows) to achieve the goal (bull's-eye).

When arrows are off-target, encourage kids to get back on-target by evaluating behavior with these three questions:

1. What could you have done differently to stay on your bull's-eye?
2. What will you do the next time?
3. What is your plan to hit your bull's-eye now?

Ask kids to think out loud, because you want to pay attention to their mental processing to pinpoint on-target and off-target thinking. Work with kids closely to choose on-target options and then aid them in constructing an action plan to hit the bull's-eye.

Teach kids to adopt this bull's-eye way of thinking by getting them to ask this question when evaluating options: "Will this choice—arrow—help me hit my bull's-eye?" Follow up immediately with this sound advice: "If the choice will keep you on target, go for it! If it won't, then find another arrow that will. Always aim for your bull's-eye by making good on-target choices." When kids are able to independently evaluate this way, they will become more skilled at choosing actions that support purpose. Moreover, they will be better able to assess the potential outcomes of their choices.

This is the purest proof of individual responsibility. It is also the most effective technique for teaching your child how to be more responsible for his choices and actions.

Most kids will take well to the concept of a bull's-eye. However, there will always be exceptions. Try it with your child to see if it helps to more effectively focus on goals, evaluate options and make responsible choices. If this approach doesn't work—for whatever reason—stick with the idea of defining purpose in terms of goals, then follow the process for teaching how to independently evaluate options and make responsible choices according to Strategy 11. What is most important is that kids learn the skill of independent evaluation.

PURPOSE Strategy 12: *Conduct periodic tune-ups.*

Your child's purpose is a product of positive traits, passions, and plans. When all of this comes together, the Hopeful Constitution and personal power materialize. This document is an accurate snapshot of who she is, what she wants, and who she aspires to be—today. I emphasize today because at some point she will change, just as her desires and dreams change. That's okay. We are supposed to change as we are exposed to new and different experiences. The little girl who wanted to be a teacher may discover that her true passion is creating with words, and now she wants to be a writer. A dimension of science a fourth-grader knew nothing about may capture his imagination in the eighth grade. A church service project may persuade a tenth grader that she wants a career in a nonprofit agency. So as your child evolves, the Hopeful Constitution will need to evolve to keep pace with changing visions and aspirations. The more in sync it is with who she is, the more value it will represent in her life. And the more value it has in her life, the more power it will have in keeping her focused on achieving her purpose. Even if goals change, the method remains the same.

As a general rule, it is recommended that you review your child's progress in achieving her positive goals at least once a week. In terms of her overall Hopeful Constitution, you would be wise to review it at least once a month. The purpose of this tune-up is not only to identify possible changes, but also to keep kids aware of strengths, passions, goals, and plans. This is important, because the more aware kids are of their purpose, the less likely they will be to stray from it. And finally, when you do sit down to conduct these periodic tune-ups, remind kids of this powerful truth: "You created your Hopeful Constitution through your choices, and only you can choose to change it." The child is not required to change the Hopeful Constitution, but he or she should know the option is available.

AT MY HOUSE

Some kids are focused from young ages. Some kids will go through phases of what they want to be when they grow up. The point of the Hopeful Constitution is to help kids see that they can control the choices that help them achieve goals, whether short-term or long-term. However, kids can change the Hopeful Constitution. That's part of their power of choice. If you resist changing the child's Hopeful Constitution because you have become attached to the child's goals, you are in effect taking away the child's power to make positive choices. So while you cannot change the Constitution yourself, neither can you block your child's choice to change it.

GINA AND ZACK, TEN YEARS LATER

Now, let's catch up with our eager examples, Gina Myers and Zack Richards, ten years after their original goals.

Gina is now twenty-four years old and living in New York City...

An unopened envelope sits noticeably by itself in the middle of a small coffee table. Gina knows the letter inside will tell her if she got the part. She has been here before, and each time she has been rejected, yet she refuses to give up her dream. Her mind begins to wander as she looks musingly upon the envelope that bears her name.

Since graduating from the New York Institute of Acting two years ago, Gina has worked as a waitress, a bartender, a bank teller, and a seamstress. Presently she is employed as a bookstore clerk. Although she has landed some leading roles in a couple of amateur plays, she has yet to get a part in a professional New York production. The competition is fierce. Nevertheless, she believes she has what it takes be a Broadway actress. Her actions attest to her will to make this happen.

On Tuesday and Thursday evenings, Gina takes acting lessons. Recently her acting coach told her about an audition for a new Broadway play. He felt she should audition for the lead character. Gina followed through with his advice and scheduled the audition. She worked hard with her coach over the next few weeks getting ready for the big day. Gina even styled her hair to look the part. She knew even the smallest details could make a big difference.

On the day of the audition, more than fifty actresses showed up. Through experience, Gina has learned to focus on her lines rather than get caught up in the competitive posturing that marks these events. She reminded herself that she was ready to do her best to get the part. Gina rehearsed her lines until the casting director called her name. A few minutes later, she was on stage, giving it her best.

The audition was challenging, but Gina felt good about her performance. Before leaving the stage, she was told, "We will inform you of our decision within a couple weeks." Experience has taught her that this is what they say to everyone, so Gina doesn't get anxious anymore. Two weeks later the letter arrived.

Rather than open it immediately, as she normally does, she takes her time to reflect on everything she has accomplished to get to where she is today and to have this opportunity. She remembers all the plays, rehearsals, hard work, college, acting seminars, rejection after rejection, and all those sacrifices. Looking at her most recent Hopeful Constitution, Gina knows she has the power to create the life she wants. Better yet, she is living the life she wants. She is thankful to be where she is and proud of her accomplishments.

Holding the unopened letter in her hand, she thinks out loud: "This cannot decide my future; only I can do that. In the worst-case scenario, it is only feedback, not failure. And no matter what it says, I know I can make it happen and create the life I want." With confidence she opens the envelope. The first thing she notices is that the letter is longer than one sentence—in fact, it is several paragraphs. Keeping her composure, she reads the first line: "Gina, please accept this letter as our offer to you to be the lead actress in our latest Broadway production. ..." The letter only gets better from there. Overcome with joy, she yells out, "Finally, yes, yes, yes!"

Hands trembling and tears flowing, Gina reaches for the phone to call her parents. It is safe to say she will accept the offer.

Zack is now twenty-two years old and living in Colorado Springs, Colorado...

The mid-morning sun burns bright, casting shadows of the buildings that Zack has called home for the past four years. Zack can't really hear what the speaker is saying. His mind is preoccupied with the memories of the people and experiences that have led him to this glorious moment. His eyes squint as he looks for his parents somewhere in the mass of onlookers. He looks down again to make sure he is holding what he has worked so hard to obtain. With white-gloved hands, he squeezes it one more time while thinking to himself, "I am really here. This is really happening."

A strong voice gets his attention. Zack has heard this voice a hundred times and knows it is time to listen. Everyone is commanded to stand. In one precise movement, a sea of blue-uniformed men and women rises. This is the moment he has dreamed about since childhood. He can barely contain his excitement. Then, just as he imagined, the words are spoken, "Congratulations. You are now commissioned officers in the United States Air Force."

Taking his hat from his head, he flings it high into the air just as his classmates do the same. For just a moment, the bright sun is blocked by what appears to be hundreds of little blue flying saucers. Emotions are high. For once, control and uniformity are replaced with spontaneity and free expression. People are hugging, crying, laughing, and sharing high-fives. Zack does his best to take it all in as he moves toward his family. And then it seizes him. Standing still, he finally realizes he has just graduated from the Air Force Academy. Holding his diploma high in the air, he loudly proclaims, "I hit my bull's-eye!"

His family gathers around him. There will be much celebrating this glorious day.

THE POWER OF PURPOSE

Gina and Zack were old enough when they learned about HOPEFUL to really see themselves as adults and stay consistent with goals they set during adolescence. This may not be true of every child. Kids develop at different rates. Hopefully the older they get, the more focused their purpose becomes in terms of education and vocation. Learning the power of purpose with small, short-term goals gives kids a valuable life-long skill.

Purpose is the expression of hope in the form of positive goals. It has the power to produce amazing results in the lives of your sons and daughters. As you work with your children to develop small goals, you will observe within them a great desire to achieve those goals. With each successful accomplishment, the desire to achieve will grow. This will lead them to the development of larger and more sophisticated goals. And as they learn to overcome obstacles and setbacks through feedback and guidance, they will begin to understand and appreciate the true meaning of cause and effect as it relates to their choices: "The quality of my outcomes is a direct result of the quality of my choices—good or bad." When kids apply this knowledge, they will have discovered the power of choice. And because they know their choices will directly influence their outcomes, they will be inspired to consciously evaluate their options before choosing a course of action. The continuation of this type of independent thinking promotes individual responsibility. Ultimately, this results in personal power—the power to create the life they want through their choices. Now they are the masters of their fate, the captains of their ships. This is the truest definition of *empowerment*.

Purposeful kids become Hopeful Kids. They grow up to be hopeful adults who may become Hopeful Parents and develop Hopeful Kids themselves. Just as purpose is the essential core of HOPEFUL, it needs to be the essential core of your children. Guide them to this purposeful way of living, and they will live a better life. And the world will be a better place to live.

PURPOSE ASSIGNMENTS

PURPOSE Assignment 4: *Play how to teach by example.*

Think of some ordinary situations that would demonstrate to your kids that the outcomes you're experiencing in your life are due to positive choices you made. For instance, on payday say, "I get this paycheck because of my positive choice to be a hardworking employee." Or, "I wanted a whole afternoon to read a novel, so I made sure I got all my chores done in the morning." In your spiral notebook, write three ways you can reinforce the power of choice by example.

PURPOSE Assignment 5: *Identify goal-oriented behaviors you will reward.*

Review your child's Hopeful Constitution. In your spiral notebook, list the specific behaviors you will be watching for so you can reward them. Check them off in your notebook as you see them and make a note of how you rewarded them.

PURPOSE Assignment 6: *Share a time you learned from feedback, not failure.*

Plan to share an experience when you faced disappointment and turned it around by thinking of it as feedback, not failure. Rehearse telling the story in a way that reinforces the principles you are trying to teach about purpose. Plan a specific time to share this experience with your kids—or one child in particular who needs to hear it. This can be during a Hopeful Hour, in the car, or throwing a ball around the yard.

PURPOSE Assignment 7: *Think out loud about a decision you face.*

Chances are you make multiple decisions every day. Choose one that would be appropriate for your children to know about, and think through your options out loud with your kids. You can do this during a casual moment over a meal or running errands together.

Hopeful Hour Planning Page

Write in your own words the main substance of Principle 3: Purpose (Part 2):

Plan how many Hopeful Hours you think you'll need to devote to this principle. List the dates you will have these Hopeful Hours. Jot down a key activity you will use in each Hopeful Hour to engage your children in learning the principle. Your activities may be suggestions you find in the chapter or adaptations you know your child will enjoy. Make sure your plan includes all the key strategies of the principle. Continue on an additional sheet of paper if necessary.

	Date	Strategy	Key Activity

CHAPTER 7

Principle 4: EXAMPLE

OBJECTIVE 4: Be a hopeful example for your child.

Children learn how to be hopeful from their parents. That's the plain and simple truth. Parents have more influence over developing hope in their kids than anyone else.

Children also learn best from example—actions over words. When kids see their parents being hopeful, they imitate and internalize what they observe. Consequently, it is what parents *do* rather than what they say that has the most powerful impact on their children. Parents, therefore, must be examples of hope—Hopeful Examples—so that their children can learn to be Hopeful Kids. The Hopeful Example attitude is: Do as I do.

So how do parents become Hopeful Examples? It is really quite simple. First, they become aware of what they *do* that encourages and discourages hopefulness in their kids. Next, they develop a plan to replace negative behaviors with hope-promoting actions. Then they do it until it becomes a habit. That's it: Awareness, Plan, and Habit.

You are probably familiar with the saying, "You are what you eat." Well, whether or not this is true is left to debate. But one thing is certain: You are what you do! That's right. You are defined more by your deeds than by your words. Respecting this truth, this section of HOPEFUL is dedicated to showing you how to make a habit out of your hope-encouraging behaviors. You will achieve this in three simple steps: 1. Awareness; 2. Action Plan; 3. Habit Formation.

The following strategies are to be completed by you, parents, outside of your family's weekly hopeful time. Every parent has a different combination of actions and habits to create, so accomplishing these strategies will take a different length of time for each person. It may be one day or it may be a few weeks. No matter what, though, get it done as soon as you can, because the sooner you get it done, the sooner you can be an example of hope for your children.

HOPEFUL TEN COMMANDMENTS

EXAMPLE Strategy 1: *Be an effective Hopeful Example by learning and applying The Hopeful Example Ten Commandments.*

I. Love your kids unconditionally.

Hopeful Examples tell their kids the three most important words every day: "I love you." They also make sure that they love their kids unconditionally. They love their kids for who they are rather than for what they do. Hopeful Examples always love their kids even when they don't love their behavior. Love the child and correct the behavior.

II. Make your kids your number one priority.

Hopeful Examples make their kids their number one priority by investing time in them and by making themselves available when their kids need them. By doing this, they greatly increase the likelihood that their kids will give them the first opportunity to help when they are upset and in need of guidance. Your priorities create your opportunities. Determine what opportunities you want from your kids, then choose your priorities accordingly.

III. Teach by example.

Hopeful Examples know that a child learns best from example. Rather than speak, they do. Their actions are constantly committed to helping their child become a Hopeful Kid by being examples of the Hopeful Motto: "I can create the life I want through positive choices and goals." Exhibit the attitude, "Do as I do." Then do as you would want your kids to do.

IV. Speak loudly with action.

Hopeful Examples understand that kids will imitate what they see before they will imitate what they hear. Words mean little; deeds mean much. A child's attitude is best summarized in this enlightening statement: "I can't hear what you are saying because your actions speak too loudly." Say less; do more.

V. Strive for excellence.

Hopeful Examples strive for excellence in all they do. Excellence is the balance point between not doing enough and doing too much. Hopeful Examples demonstrate excellence toward their children by giving their best effort to helping them become Hopeful Kids. Don't settle for less than excellent execution.

VI. Fulfill your promises.

Hopeful Examples fully understand the importance of fulfilling their promises. In all cases, their most important promise is to help their child become a Hopeful Kid. Keeping this foremost in their minds, they do their best to make this happen by using HOPEFUL. Keep your promises.

VII. Apologize when you make a mistake.

Hopeful Examples are conscious of how their actions influence a child's life. At times, they fall short of their intended desire to help. And still other times, they just plain blow it. When this happens, Hopeful

Examples genuinely apologize for the negative way they have affected their son or daughter, then they make immediate and genuine efforts to reconcile the wrongdoing. Kids expect an apology when a parent makes a mistake. Acknowledge your mistakes with two words: "I'm sorry."

VIII. Evaluate your options.

Hopeful Examples know that when they choose an action, they also choose the consequences of that action—good or bad. Because of this, Hopeful Examples carefully evaluate their options before they make a choice and initiate action. They do this by asking one question when dealing with issues related to their son or daughter: "Will this encourage my kid's hopeful growth?" If the answer is yes, they go for it. If it is no, they move on to find other options that will promote hope. This conscious approach to decision-making results in responsible choices that reinforce their child's hopeful development. Think. Choose. Act.

IX. Respect all people.

Hopeful Examples commit themselves to valuing others no matter what their race, gender, age, status or physical being. They practice this approach with their children by respecting individuality and viewpoint even when they disagree. By doing this, they are proving by example that kids matter and that what they have to say is important. By following parents' examples, kids will learn to respect themselves and others. Give respect to get respect.

X. Live hopefully.

Hopeful Examples make sure their actions constantly support the Hopeful Motto: "I can create the life I want through positive choices and goals." They understand it, believe it, and ultimately they live it! Their children see this and learn how to be hopeful through replication. "Live as you would want your children to live."

At this point you should have a solid understanding of what it takes to be a Hopeful Example for your kid. And just in case you are wondering, every parent, including you, is more than capable of applying all of these hope-encouraging actions and commandments to a child's life. Make sure to include them in your growing repertoire of hope-inspiring skills. Learn them, apply them, live them.

Okay, it's time to develop your Hopeful Example Action Plan. Next, you will learn how to turn it into a hopeful habit. As you know, you will accomplish this in three easy steps: 1. Awareness; 2. Action Plan; 3. Habit Formation.

EXAMPLE Strategy 2. Awareness: *Be a more conscious and influential Hopeful Example by identifying your hope-encouraging and hope-discouraging behaviors.*

Our objective here is to make you highly aware of what you do that encourages and discourages hopefulness in your son or daughter. By making you conscious of these behaviors, you will be more apt to display those actions that promote hopefulness. This awareness will help you to become a more effective Hopeful Example.

Set aside thirty minutes to an hour to complete this exercise. You will need a sheet of notebook paper and a pen or pencil. Draw a vertical line down the middle of the paper. On the top left side of the paper, write this title: "Hope Encouragement." Label the right side "Hope Discouragement."

Beginning with "Hope Encouragement," brainstorm every behavior you exhibit toward your child that encourages hopeful development based on the Hopeful Constitution and the Hopeful Motto: "I can create the life I want through positive choices and goals." List everything that comes to mind. Examples of such hopeful actions would include:

- being open
- recognizing your kid's ability to make positive choices
- supporting your child's positive activities and goals
- spending time with your kid
- making yourself available when your child needs you

- encouraging your child to assertively express feelings when upset
- reinforcing your child's positive traits
- rewarding your kid's behavior for staying on-target and achieving a goal
- …and everything else you do that promotes hopefulness.

This should take about ten minutes, but spend as much time as you need to identify all of your hope-encouraging behaviors.

Now go to the right side of the paper and identify every action you exhibit toward your child that discourages hopeful development. Even though you may find this difficult, it is crucial that you are genuinely open with yourself. Only you will know what you have written, and only you will see this list. However, if there are two parents involved, you will need to share and compare your lists in order to help one another identify hope-promoting behaviors to replace hope-demoting behaviors. Give this your best, most genuine effort because awareness is the first step to change. Again, give yourself about ten to fifteen minutes to complete this task. Here are some examples of hope-discouraging behaviors:

- yelling when you are upset
- saying hurtful things when you are mad that you don't mean
- being physically aggressive when you are angry
- lacking interest in your kid's activities
- failing to listen when your child wants to talk with you
- pointing out your child's short-comings
- insensitive teasing that causes your kid to get upset
- talking down to your child
- disrespecting your kid when she is with her friends
- not supporting your child's dreams or goals
- failing to follow through with your commitments or promises.

Now, for the next ten minutes or so, group similar actions and behaviors into short phrases for both lists. For example, Hope Encouragement:

"Spending time with my daughter"; Hope Discouragement: "Not supporting my son's goals." Next, determine the top five encouraging and discouraging behaviors you exhibit most often. On a separate piece of paper with the same headings (Hope Encouragement and Hope Discouragement) list these top five behaviors from most frequent to least frequent. To give you an idea of what your list might look like when it is finished, here is an example of what Jason created. You should remember Jason as the single father who assertively resolved an issue with his daughter Nicki, during Principle 2: OPEN.

HOPE ENCOURAGEMENT

1. Reinforcing my kids' strengths.
2. Supporting my kids' goals.
3. Being open with them.
4. Making time when they need me.
5. Teaching and being assertive.

HOPE DISCOURAGEMENT

1. Yelling when I get mad.
2. Not listening sometimes.
3. Talking down to my kids.
4. Forcing them to do it my way.
5. Saying mean things when I get mad.

When you have created your list, you are ready for the second step in this process: Action Plan.

EXAMPLE Strategy 3. Action Plan: *Strengthen and increase the frequency of your hope-encouraging behaviors by developing a Hopeful Example Action Plan.*

In this strategy you will learn how to overcome your hope-discouraging behaviors by replacing them with your hope-encouraging behaviors. You will accomplish this objective by creating a Hopeful Example Action Plan.

Take the list you created in the previous step and prepare to write some sentences. These sentences will effectively strengthen your inspiring actions while simultaneously neutralizing your discouraging tendencies. Remember, for every negative there is a positive. Put this into practice by replacing each of your negative actions with hope-promoting, positive actions. Below is the sentence template you will use to compose each of your hope-affirming statements:

When I feel _____
                    (write hope-discouragement behavior here).

I will be a Hopeful Example by _____

_____
                    (write hope-encouragement behavior here).

Basically, your intent here is to hire your positive behaviors and fire your negative ones. Begin with your first negative, then find a positive to replace it. Continue this process until you find a positive replacement for each negative behavior you listed. It doesn't matter which positive behaviors you choose as long as they motivate you to exhibit hopeful behavior toward your son or daughter. This is how you will learn to be a Hopeful Example. If there isn't an encouraging behavior on your list to replace the discouraging one, then you need to find one that will work. Should this be the case, feel free to use any of the Hopeful Example Ten Commandments or anything else you have learned from HOPEFUL in order to find a positive replacement. Remember, for every negative there is a positive.

Referring back to Jason's list, here is the action plan he created. Notice how he has gone beyond his original list to find other hope-encouraging strategies to replace his negative behaviors. Also, take note of how he puts a little more effort into documenting how he will implement these specific strategies as part of his overall plan.

MY HOPEFUL EXAMPLE ACTION PLAN

1. When I feel like yelling when I am mad, I will be a Hopeful Example by openly expressing my feelings assertively. If I am really mad, I will Take Ten or as long as I need to get back in control. Yelling gets me nowhere. Only I can choose my reaction: Think. Choose. Act.

2. When I feel like I am not listening to my kids, I will be a Hopeful

Example by focusing my attention on them. I will make sure to practice the three Rs of open communication: receive, respect and respond. If they need to talk with me, I will make time to listen. If it isn't urgent and I am in a hurry, I will let them know that I am in a rush and that I will make time to talk with them later.

3.   When I feel like I am getting ready to talk down to my kids, I will be a Hopeful Example by believing in them and reinforcing their strengths and goals: Believe it—get it. If I expect my kids to respect me, I need to give respect to get it.

4.   When I feel like I am getting ready to force my kids to do it my way, I will be a Hopeful Example by supporting my kids' strengths. I will ask them how they think they should do it, then listen to their answer. If I feel it is off-target, I will be open about my feelings, then work with them to find a way to get back on target. Also, I have to remember that my kids are going to make mistakes, but mistakes are their best teachers. Feedback, not failure.

5.   When I feel like I am getting ready to say mean things to my kids when I am mad, I will be a Hopeful Example by openly expressing my feelings. If I am too angry, I will tell my kids that I need a break and that I will return to the issue later. No matter what, though, I will stay in control.

Finish your plan with this statement (note: the hope-encouraging behaviors are from Jason's list):

I will do my best to be a Hopeful Example by following The Hopeful Example Ten Commandments and by demonstrating my hope-encouraging behaviors:

1.   Reinforcing my kids' strengths.
2.   Supporting my kids' goals.
3.   Being open with them.
4.   Making time when they need me.
5.   Teaching and being assertive.

There you go. You have just developed your very own Hopeful Example Action Plan. Make sure to keep it with your child's Hopeful Constitution. Now you are ready to make it a habit.

EXAMPLE Strategy 4. Habit Formation: *Be an effective Hopeful Example for your children by converting your hope-encouraging behaviors into a hopeful habit.*

Previously you learned that it takes thirty days to form a habit. What this really means is that in order for a new behavior to become a habit, you have to do it for thirty consecutive days. Now, let's apply this habit-forming strategy to your plan.

- First, you will need a calendar or appointment book that has each of the next thirty days clearly displayed. Write the term "Hopeful Example" on each of these days.
- Next, read your Hopeful Example Action Plan and the Hopeful Example Ten Commandments every morning and evening for the next thirty consecutive days.
- Carry your action plan with you every day, wherever you go. You can keep it with your appointment book, in your back pocket, wallet, purse, or wherever else it will be with you all day. Remember to read it at least once during the day: breaks, lunch, on the train, etc.
- Say this sentence to yourself prior to every interaction with your children: "I will do my best to be a Hopeful Example."
- Just before you go to bed, place a check mark or X on the day you just completed. Remember to read your plan and Ten Commandments.
- Last, assess your performance at the end of each day by asking yourself three questions:

    1. What worked?
    2. What didn't work?
    3. What will I do the next time?

Your answers to these questions will help you to quickly identify effective and ineffective actions. Ultimately, repeat behaviors that encourage hope and replace behaviors that discourage hope. You are now prepared for the next day.

Presto! Follow this habit-formation recipe and you will soon become a living, breathing Hopeful Example. At the end of the thirty days, review your action plan and determine if you need to make any changes. Keep it current by updating it every time you tune up your son or daughter's Hopeful Constitution or any time you feel you are not being an effective Hopeful Example.

EXAMPLE: JASON AND DEVIN

Okay, let's see how Jason uses these strategies to be an example of hope for his son. Let's join Jason in the fourth week of becoming a Hopeful Example. As you recall, he is a single father of two children: Nicki age fifteen (whom you met earlier) and Devin, age eight. What follows is a demonstration of how Jason effectively used his hope-encouraging behaviors to be a Hopeful Example for Devin during a critical moment.

It's a beautiful Sunday morning. Jason is on his way to join a couple friends for their weekly round of golf. Nicki is babysitting Devin until their mother, Jason's former wife, picks Devin up to take him to a friend's birthday party. While backing out of the driveway, he notices Devin rushing toward the car frantically waving his arms and yelling. Shifting the car into park, Jason rolls down the window and asks, "What's wrong?" Devin does his best to try to talk but is overcome with emotion. Jason tells him to Take Ten to gather himself.

> Jason: Can you tell me what happened now?"
> Devin: (still upset, but in better control) I called Mom to make sure she wasn't going to be late. Then she told me

she couldn't pick me up—again! This is the third time she
has done this. She promised to take me to my friend's birthday
party. She never keeps her promises! Now I have no way of
getting to the party.

Jason: (calmly) Why can't your mom make it?

Devin: Because she was drunk! She could barely talk. She
didn't even remember she was supposed to pick me up.
Dad, I really need you right now!

Hearing these words, Jason knows he needs to make time to
listen and to focus his attention on Devin. *There will be other golf games. I
need to do my best to be a Hopeful Example for Devin right now*, he thinks
to himself as he gets out of the car and kneels next to Devin.

Jason: If you need me, I am here for you. Do you want to
talk out here or in the house?

Devin: I don't care. Dad, can you make Mom get out of
bed and come get me? I've been looking forward to this
party forever.

Jason: I am sorry your mom did this. But I don't think talking to her right now is going to make any difference. No
one can make her change. Only she can choose to make
that happen. And until she makes that choice, she will continue to do this kind of thing.

Devin: (dejected) What do I do now?

Jason: You know how to make good choices, so what do
you think your options are right now?

Devin: Well, I could try to get a ride with some of my other
friends, but I still need one of my parents to be there with
me. So I guess that won't work. Nicki can't drive yet, plus
she isn't one of my parents. That won't work either. The only
other person is you, but I know today is your golf day.

Jason: (puts his hand on his son's shoulder) Do you

remember when I told you that if you needed me, I would
be there for you?
Devin: Yeah.
Jason: Good. It sounds like this is very important to you.
Devin: It is!
Jason: Golf can wait another week, but it doesn't sound
like this party can.
Devin: No.
Jason: Well, we'd better hurry up if we don't want to miss
the cake.

Devin ran to the house to get his bathing suit while happily yelling,
"All right! I get to go! I get to go!" Jason then calls his friends to let them
know that he won't be golfing today. As Devin gets in the car, Jason says:

Jason: Devin, anytime you want to talk with me about your
mom, I will make the time to listen. Just let me know.
Devin: I know. Maybe later. Right now all I want to do is to
get to the party.

Jason starts the car, then cheerfully offers, "What are we waiting
for? Let's go." It's a beautiful Sunday morning. Father and son are off to a
birthday party.

You are undoubtedly familiar with this phrase: "A picture is
worth a thousands words." Well, the same can be said for a single deed.
An action is worth a thousand words. You say more with your behavior
than you could ever say with your words.

Hopeful Parents are Hopeful Examples because they believe and
live the Hopeful Motto: "I can create the life I want through positive choices
and goals." In turn, their kids imitate their parent's example. Simply said,
hopefulness begets hopefulness. Thus, Hopeful Parents develop Hopeful
Kids. Result: a Hopeful Generation—one kid and one family at a time.

EXAMPLE ASSIGNMENTS

EXAMPLE Assignment 1: *Learn the Ten Hopeful Commandments.*

Make your own written copy of the Hopeful 10 Commandments. Use just the key phrases as reminders of the commandments. 1. Love your kids unconditionally. 2. Make your kids your number one priority. 3. Teach by example. 4. Speak loudly with action. 5. Strive for excellence. 6. Fulfill your promises. 7. Apologize when you make a mistake. 8. Evaluate your options. 9. Respect all people. 10. Live hopefully.

Learn these commandments to the point that you can repeat these key phrases. Use them as a guide for your interactions with your kids.

EXAMPLE Assignment 2: *Make your Hopeful Example Action Plan.*

Schedule an hour of undisturbed time to create your very own Hopeful Example Action Plan (see Strategies 2 and 3). This will give you a head start on promoting your child's hopeful development while you finish reading the remaining key principles. Remember, Hopeful Parents develop Hopeful Kids by example. Great example of cause-and-effect!

EXAMPLE Assignment 3: *Form a hopeful habit.*

Prepare a calendar as outlined in Strategy 4 and work consistently on converting your hope-encouraging behaviors into habits.

HOPEFUL HOUR PLANNING PAGE

Write in your own words the main substance of Principle 4: EXAMPLE:

Plan how many Hopeful Hours you think you'll need to devote to this principle. List the dates you will have these Hopeful Hours. Jot down a key activity you will use in each Hopeful Hour to engage your children in learning the principle. Your activities may be suggestions you find in the chapter or adaptations you know your child will enjoy. Make sure your plan includes all the key strategies of the principle. Continue on an additional sheet of paper if necessary.

	Date	Strategy	Key Activity

CHAPTER 8

Principle 5: FIND

OBJECTIVE 5: Teach your child how to find solutions.

Why does a child seek help from a parent? Most likely because she is facing a problem of some sort—a toy that is stuck, a shoe untied, difficult homework, being bullied at school, a falling-out with a friend. A problem exists when a child doesn't know how to respond to a situation and this creates some degree of stress. In other words, the presenting demand exceeds her present resources, which causes her to feel challenged or frustrated. Believe it or not, these ongoing challenges are essential to a young person's maturation and development. When a problem creates stress, a child is compelled to find the resources to solve the problem. Learning how to do this effectively and consistently will increase her coping skills, thereby helping her gain greater mastery over her environment. Consequently, the child will become that much more capable of creating the life she wants.

On the other hand, when a young person is unable to effectively solve problems, the weight and severity of the problems can cause significant stress. If this continues without intervention, hopelessness will take residence. Obviously, the key to preventing this from happening to your child is to teach her how to find solutions.

Unresolved problems promote hopelessness. When we are able to effectively find solutions, we are better able to manage our lives toward hopeful ends. Problem-solving skills are necessary to living a hopeful life. Hence, Principle 5 is dedicated to showing you how to find solutions with a highly effective problem-solving method known simply as D-BEST.

FIND STRATEGIES

FIND Strategy 1: *Learn the D-BEST method to systematically problem-solve and find solutions.*

The quality of the method determines the quality of the result. Or, put another way, an effective problem-solving method results in effective solutions.

Each time we successfully solve a problem, we incrementally increase our resources to resolve future challenges. That is to say, we improve our capacity to cope with future problems. The key to doing this effectively and consistently, however, lies more in the method than anything else. People who know how to solve problems are better able to manage and enjoy their lives than those who do not. Hopeful Parents understand this truth, and as a result they teach their kids how to find solutions with a simple yet extremely effective problem-solving method know as D-BEST. And as you have probably already guessed, each letter represents a distinct step in the problem-solving process:

D = Define the problem: who, what, when, where, why (five W's) and how?

B = Brainstorm options to solve the problem.
E = Evaluate the options until a potential solution is found.
S = Select the best options.
T = Test the options to determine if they solve the problem.

Before we get started, it is worth reminding you that we teach best by example. So as we go through the steps of D-BEST, be thinking about how they apply to a challenge that you face. One of the Find Assignments will be to use this method to find a solution to one of your problems. Then plan how you will teach your children the method during Hopeful Hour. Here's an overview of the system.

D = DEFINE the problem: who, what, when, where, why and how?
There can be no solution without a well-defined problem. That is why it is so important to clearly define the problem in terms of who, what, when, where, why (the five W's once again) and how? Once you understand the problem, you are well on your way to solving it. Below is a sample list of the questions you would ask in order to define a problem:

What is the problem?
Who is involved in the problem?
When does the problem occur?
Where does the problem occur?
Why does the problem occur?
How does the problem occur?

Make sure to ask all of these questions when you are first defining a problem. Because every problem is different, some of these questions will apply while others will not, but you'll sort that out as you ask the questions. Also, you may have to work a little to find answers to these questions. That's okay, because the time you invest here will give you tremendous insight into the cause of the problem. Ultimately, this insight will lead you to develop a more effective solution. Keep this in mind: A problem that is well defined is half solved.

B = BRAINSTORM options to solve the problem.

The goal of brainstorming is to identify as many potential options as possible to solve the problem. You will do this by listing each idea as it pops into your head until every potential solution is exhausted. Don't worry about whether or not an idea will actually work; just get it down. You will evaluate each option's viability to solve the problem in the next step.

E = EVALUATE the options until a potential solution is found.

This is where you will determine if an option has the potential to solve the problem. Evaluate every listed option by asking this question: "How effective will this option be in helping us to solve the problem?" Do this until you have identified and prioritized the options that seem most promising.

S = SELECT the best options.

Based on your list of the most viable options, select the ones you believe will solve the problem. Once they are selected, each person involved in solving the problem will receive specific assignments. You will determine who will do what, when, where and how? Only ask "why" questions if the assignment doesn't seem to promote the achievement of the solution. If this is the case, revise the assignment until it fits with the desired outcome. Ultimately, everyone involved in solving the problem should be clear on what he or she is expected to do to achieve the desired solution. Next, schedule a date to determine if the assigned action is working based on the next step.

T = TEST the options to determine if they solve the problem.

This is where the options and assignments are put to the test. Each person will be expected to test the effectiveness of his or her assignments to achieve the desired solution. Ask this question: "Is your assignment helping you to solve the problem?" If the answer is yes, the person continues with the assigned action until the problem is solved. If the answer is no, identify a new option to be tested. This process continues until the problem is solved.

At My House

> Use this space to briefly describe a problem you face and plan to use D-BEST to solve it.
>
> _____
>
> _____
>
> _____
>
> _____
>
> _____
>
> _____

Find Strategy 2: *Teach the D-BEST method during Hopeful Hour.*

Conduct this problem-solving exercise during your Hopeful Hour. Begin by telling your child that you want to show him how to solve problems by using a very simple method called D-BEST. Go on to explain that problems are a normal part of life and that everyone has them. The key, however, is learning how to solve them effectively and consistently. Let your kid know that learning how to do this will help him create the life he wants. Here is a simple way to get this message across:

It is okay to have problems. Everyone does. What isn't okay, though, is not knowing how to solve them. That is why I am going to show you how to solve your problems the best (D-BEST) way. This will help you create the life you want.

If your children are eight or younger, it may be helpful to spend some time making sure they understand what a problem is. This is the simplest statement to define a problem: "A problem happens when you don't know what to do about someone or something." Try to get kids to identify some of their own real-life problems. It may also be helpful to share some of your own problems about someone and something that kids can identify with and comprehend.

Next, on a piece of paper, have kids list all of the problems they are facing at this present moment. Depending on your kids' ages, examples may include a broken bike, poor grades, a difficult teacher, a dispute with a friend, a difficult classmate, a recent break-up with a boyfriend, a lack of money to buy something she wants, a difficult boss, problems with you, a heath problem, a car that needs work—or any number of other problems. Once the list is complete, have each child identify his or her top three problems. These should be people, events, or things that are causing the greatest level of stress because kids don't know *how* to solve them. Have kids list these problems from most urgent to least urgent on a page in the Hopeful Kid's Notebook titled "My Problems."

HOPEFUL HOUR TIP

 Depending on the age and development of your children, they may need assistance in identifying problems. It might help to give some examples of problems that have occurred in your family recently. Make a brief list ahead of time of things you might mention to help children get going. Also, don't cast judgment on anything kids say. Someone might mention something that sounds trivial to others in the family, as if it's not really a problem, but it might be something that causes true stress for the person who mentioned it. This is not the time to make those evaluations. Focus on teaching the method, no matter how small or how big the problem seems.

You may be surprised by what your child lists as problems. Sometimes a young person is more comfortable writing something down as opposed to expressing it verbally. In the event you should see something that causes you grave concern, the first thing you must do is keep your cool! Your first reaction will significantly influence your child's reaction. Also, by maintaining your composure, demonstrate the importance of keeping a level head when it comes to solving problems. The next thing you need to do is to confidently tell your child that you will do everything you can to help find a solution.

Starting with the number one problem on your child's list, begin showing how to apply the D-BEST method. Go over each of the five steps until kids understand what they mean in relation to helping to find solutions. If you've applied D-BEST to a problem you face, you'll be able to give some examples. Or you could tell the story of the Wilson family (below) to illustrate the D-BEST steps. Walk each child through the process with at least one problem from that child's list. Give as much input or as many suggestions as necessary to help the child grasp the concept of each step. Then with the next problem, give less input and suggestions and see if your child can be more independent. You can work on this during Hopeful Hours or at any time you have an opportunity to check in with a child about a problem.

HOPEFUL HOUR TIP

Depending on how many kids you're working with and the depth of the problems that emerge from this discussion, you may not be able to apply D-BEST to a problem for every child in one session. If problems seem pressing, however, plan to spend some extra time giving each child the attention he or she needs. Asking a child to wait a week or two to get help may cause discouragement.

FIND Strategy 3: *Encourage a habit of using D-BEST.*

Here are some final pointers on how to teach and encourage your sons and daughters to find solutions:

- Make problem solving with D-BEST a habit in your family.
- Have older kids carry D-BEST with them on 3 x 5 cards.
- Periodically ask if kids have any problems they want to work on.
- Get your child to the point where he or she can use D-BEST independently.
- Prove to your child that D-BEST works by using it to solve your own problems.
- Find and ask for help if you don't know how to solve a problem.

A family that finds solutions together finds hopefulness together. And each time your kid sees you solve a problem using this method, she will become that much more convinced that she can do the same. Furthermore, each time she experiences success using this method, she will become that much more capable of solving her own problems independently.

Most of the time, you will know how to help your child with a serious problem. However, it is a fact of life that despite your best effort, there will be those times, for whatever reason, you will *not* know how to help your child. Life is just too complex and unpredictable for you to know how to handle everything your kid will encounter. That is okay, because there are a great multitude of dedicated people and resources that are ready, willing, and able to help your family. You can take comfort in the fact that what you don't know how to do, someone else does. All it takes is some effort.

That's right, through a little effort on your part, you can find the help your son or daughter needs to resolve the problem. We live in the most resource-rich country in the world! Throughout the United States, there are literally thousands upon thousands of people, agencies, and related resources that are ready to provide the help your family needs whenever you need it. Best of all, most of these helpful people and organizations can be easily accessed for little or no money. This is because they are funded by private and public sources that want to help people—you and your child— live a better life. The main thing is to remember that you don't have to go through it alone. Agencies are full of real people who want to help.

And finally, parents, listen up: If you have a serious problem— depression, alcohol/drug abuse, domestic violence, gambling—you need to do the same for yourself: find and ask for help! Show your child that it's okay to get help when you don't know what to do. Remember: those who ask for help get help; those who don't, don't!

Now, let's see how the Wilson's put D-BEST to work for their family.

THE WILSON FAMILY USES D-BEST

You'll remember the Wilson family from Principle 1: HOUR, where they worked together to create their Hopeful Hour schedule. The parents, Carl and Tina Wilson, have two sons: Jimmy, age nine, and Sam, age eleven. Recently during their Family Time, Carl and Tina were teaching the boys how to problem-solve with D-BEST. When they got to the part where they had their sons list their present problems, they immediately took notice of the lone problem Sam listed: "Someone wants to hurt me." Needless to say, the parents were startled. Here is what transpired over the next hour, as well as the next few days:

> Tina: *(looking at Carl)* Okay, okay, let's keep our cool and find out what is going on here. *(turning to Sam)* What is this all about?
>
> Sam: *(fidgeting with his pencil)* I didn't want to say anything because I didn't want you to think I couldn't handle this by myself. But I don't want to go to school because there is another boy who picks on me.

Carl: (getting angry) Who is picking on you? I'll call the principal and handle this right now!

Tina: (places her hand on Carl's knee) Let's remember to keep cool.

Carl: (Takes Ten to calm down and regain his composure) First of all, your mom and I will do everything we can to make sure that you aren't bullied at school. Do you understand that, Sam?

Sam: Yeah.

Carl: We are going to solve this problem right now. (looking at Sam) Are you ready?

Sam: (holding back tears) I think so. I mean … I don't know what else to do.

Carl: (places arm around Sam and uses confident tone) You are doing the right thing. And we are all here to help you solve this problem and to make sure you don't get hurt!

Tina: Sam, I know you are scared. You should be and anyone in your shoes would be. But you need to hear me when I tell you this: There is no way we are going to let this bullying continue. Do you hear what I am saying to you?

Sam: Yes

Tina: (looking at Jimmy) Do you understand what is going on right now?

Jimmy: I don't want anything to happen to Sam! This guy is really mean and he has hurt people before! Everyone is scared of him—even the teachers!

Tina: Sam, it's okay to be scared, especially when someone says he is going to hurt you. But what isn't okay is trying to handle this all by yourself when you don't know what to do. Everyone needs help when something like this happens. So first of all, we are very proud of you for coming to us for help. And Jimmy, we want you to do the same if this were ever to happen to you. All right, let's get this thing figured out.

Carl then tells the boys that the first thing he and Tina are going to do is explain how the D-BEST method works, then apply it to Sam's problem to find a solution. Carl and Tina go over the five steps of D-BEST, then make sure Jimmy and Sam understand what each step means in the problem-solving process.

Tina: Eventually you will be able to use D-BEST all by yourself to solve your problems. And when you can't solve a problem, we want you to ask us for help so we can help you find a solution, just like we are doing right now. Do you understand what I just said?

Jimmy: Yes.

Sam: I didn't know there was such a thing as "problem-solving." It sounds pretty simple with this D-BEST thing. I just hope it will help me solve my problem.

Carl: Your mom and I use this to solve our problems when we don't know what to do. It has helped us every time. Finding solutions is not always easy. Sometimes it takes a lot of work. The important thing is that you give it your best shot. At least D-BEST makes it a lot easier because it lays out the steps you have to go through to solve a problem. Remember, everyone has problems. They're a fact of life. The most important thing, though, is that you learn how to solve them. That is why your mom and I are teaching you how to do this with D-BEST. Eventually you will be able to do this on your own. And once you know how to solve your problems independently, you will live a happier life. Okay, let's put it to work on this problem.

APPLYING D-BEST TO SAM'S PROBLEM

D = DEFINE the problem: who, what, when, where, why (five Ws) and how:

Carl: You already said what your problem was when you told us that *someone wants to hurt you*. Now we need to ask you a few more questions to really understand your problem. The first question we have for you is, who said this to you?

Sam: This kid by the name of Markus. He's a couple years older than me, and he's in the eighth grade. He's always causing trouble at school. He stole my backpack and is always making threats if I don't give him what he wants.

Tina: Have you told anyone else that he threatened you?

Sam: No. I didn't know who to go to, and I didn't want people to think I was scared. But now that we have talked about this, I know it's okay to be scared. I'm just glad I finally came to you so that you can help me.

Carl: There is no doubt that we are going to get to the bottom of this and help you. Sam, you are doing the right thing by coming to us for help. Now, when and where did Markus last threaten you?

Sam: It happened last Friday in the school cafeteria during lunch.

Tina: Okay. So how did this happen?

Sam: I was carrying my lunch tray toward the trash-can when, all of a sudden, I bumped into Markus as he was getting up from his table. I didn't see him until it was too late. When I bumped into him, the rest of my milk spilled on the front of his shirt. Some people started to laugh, and then I knew I was in big trouble. I told him I was sorry, but he didn't care. He grabbed me by my collar and said, "If you don't bring me $10 tomorrow, I'm going to beat you up." I was really afraid and pulled away from him. He tried to grab me again, but I ran away.

Tina: Did any teachers see what happened?

Sam: No, so I just went to my next class. When it was out, I made sure he wasn't around before I went to my last class. For the last two days, Monday and Tuesday, I have been looking for him before I go anywhere at school. And today one of his friends, Smitty, told me that Markus was going to get me eventually.

Carl: Man, it seems like these guys don't know when to let it go. All right, we are almost done. One more question: Why would he want to fight with you over such a small thing?

Sam: I don't know. He's just like that. Everyone at school knows he is a hothead. Teachers hate dealing with him. He's been kicked out of school for fighting, but they keep letting him come back. And every time he comes back, he brags about how no one can tell him what to do.

Carl: Hmm, that's too bad. Is that everything?

Sam: Yeah, that's all I know.

Tina: Well, it sounds like you didn't provoke this situation and that Markus is a very angry young man. So let's make sure we understand the problem: Markus threatened to fight with you last Friday, after you accidentally spilled some milk on him, unless you gave him $10 the next day. Also, no teachers or staff saw what happened. You have been looking out for him ever since. And on Tuesday, his friend Smitty told you that Markus was going to get you. Does that sound about right?

Sam: Yep. That's what happened. Basically, I am afraid that Markus is going to beat me up.

Carl: Sam, we will not let that happen to you! We are going to solve this problem and do our best to prevent Markus from hurting you. Okay, now that we understand what happened, it is time to move on to step 2 in D-BEST—Brainstorm.

B = BRAINSTORM options to solve the problem:

Tina begins by telling everyone that the objective in this stage of problem-solving is to *brainstorm* as many options as possible to help solve the problem. Sam asked her what brainstorming meant. She explained it like this:

Tina: Brainstorming means that we work together to identify and list every potential solution that we think will help solve the problem. It doesn't matter if the idea will actually work or not. The main thing is that we get it down while we are thinking about it. We will determine which options are the best for solving this problem in the next step—*Evaluate*.

The Wilson family then spent the next ten minutes listing every possible solution that each family member had to offer until no more options could be identified. Carl wrote down each potential solution as it was brainstormed. Next, they joined like ideas together until they had the following list of options:

- Quit going to school or change schools.
- Talk to the principal, Mr. Jenkins.
- Talk to Markus.
- Talk to Markus's parents.
- Apologize to Markus again for bumping into him.
- Tell the teachers what is going on.

Now the Wilson's are ready to move on to the third stage of the D-BEST process—Evaluate.

E = EVALUATE the options until a potential solution is found:

In this stage, the Wilson family will evaluate each of their brainstormed options to determine which ones will be the most effective in helping the family solve Sam's problem. Carl directs this process by having each family member, including himself, offer his or her evaluation of each option, one by one, to solve the problem. Before evaluating each option, Carl asked the family this question: "How effective will this option be in helping us solve the problem?" Below is a summary of what the Wilsons determined for each option:

- *Quit going to school or change schools.*

The family agreed that this was not a viable option for the simple reason that Sam needed to go to school in order to get an education. Further, Sam couldn't avoid problems in life by simply running away from bullies. Changing schools was simply running away. What the family did decide, however, was that Sam would not attend school until they had a meeting with the principal and to develop a viable plan to solve the problem immediately.

- *Talk to the principal, Mr. Jenkins.*

The Wilsons were in total agreement that Mr. Jenkins should be made aware of the problem, not only for Sam's safety, but also for the safety of everyone on campus. Just as important, the family believed that Mr. Jenkins was in the best position to guide Markus and his family to getting the help they needed.

- *Talk to Markus.*

The parents have taught their sons to try to talk their problems out and to walk away if it looks like someone wants to fight. But because Markus has threatened to hurt Sam, the parents feel that any attempt to talk with Markus would only escalate the situation and put Sam in harm's way. They believe the only people that should be talking to Markus are the principal and his parents.

- *Talk to Markus's parents.*

Carl and Tina would have no problem having an open discussion with another child's parents to resolve a problem. This would be one viable option.

- *Apologize to Markus again for bumping into him.*

Again, the family does not believe this is a worthwhile option for the same reasons that talking to Markus is ill-advised. Plus, Sam already attempted to apologize to Markus when he first bumped into him in the school cafeteria with no positive results.

- *Tell the teachers what is going on.*

Sam agrees that he should have talked to his teachers as soon as the incident happened. However, now that the situation has escalated, the family believes the best option is to talk to the principal first to see what they recommend.

   S = SELECT the best options.
   Carl introduced the fourth step of D-BEST with this statement: "Now that we have evaluated our options, it is time to select the best ones." Based on their previous evaluation, the Wilson family believes the following options offer the best approach for solving Sam's problem:

- Talk to Markus's parents.
- Talk to the principal, Mr. Jenkins.

Now that the best possible solutions have been selected, Tina tells the family it is time to determine who will do what, when, where, and how, as well as set a review date to determine if the options are working. Remember, the family asks "why" only if a proposed assignment doesn't seem to support the desired solution. When they finish this process, they agree to the following assignments:

- *Talk to Markus's parents.*
   It is decided that Carl, Tina, and Sam will go to the school to get the contact information for Markus's parents the very next morning. Jimmy will go to school. Carl and Tina will take time off from work to deal with this very important situation.

- *Talk to the principal, Mr. Jenkins.*
It is decided that Tina will call Mr. Jenkins first thing in the morning to make an appointment to see him about Sam's serious problem. Tina and Carl will escort Sam to school to meet with Mr. Jenkins.

   The family agrees to review their progress tomorrow evening. Now it is time to apply these potential solutions to the fifth and final stage of D-BEST—Test.

T = TEST the options to determine if they solve the problem:

The next morning, Tina calls Mr. Jenkins. He is very concerned and determined to get the problem resolved. He makes room in his busy schedule to meet with the family at 11:30 a.m. Mr. Jenkins goes on to say that he will also call Markus's parents and tell them the situation about their son.

The Wilsons arrive on school grounds at 11:30 a.m. They are immediately escorted to Mr. Jenkins's office. When everyone is seated, Mr. Jenkins advises the family that the school has suspended Markus because there were three other students who witnessed the episode in the cafeteria and signed statements verifying the threats to Sam. He went on to say, "Markus will be suspended from school for five days and will be watched by a safe-schools officer when he returns." Relieved, Sam lets out a sigh of relief.

Mr. Jenkins then says to him "Sam, you are a brave young man, and because of you, this school is a safer place." Continuing, he sincerely adds, "We are extremely grateful that you and your family had the courage to come forward and deal with this problem."

Next, Mr. Jenkins recommends that Sam return to school the following day. Also, he lets the family know that a school social worker will be made available to meet with them should they choose to do so.

Before concluding the meeting, Sam asks about Markus's friend Smitty.

Mr. Jenkins boldly offers these reassuring words. "After Markus was suspended, we suspended Smitty for one day and talked to his parents about the situation. We will have a required parent conference with them before Smitty is allowed to return to school. Smitty knows that if he threatens or harasses you or anyone else ever again, he will be immediately suspended again. In fact, he and his parents will have to sign an agreement to this effect before he is readmitted. It is clear that Smitty's parents are very concerned about what has happened, and they, as well as Smitty, have assured us that this will never happen again. I don't think he will cause any more problems, but just in case he does, just let me know, and we will deal with it immediately. Keeping everyone safe is my number one priority.

Satisfied with Mr. Jenkins response, Sam declares, "What a relief to know that I can come back to school and not have to worry about getting hurt by Markus anymore." The meeting concludes with Carl and Tina thanking Mr. Jenkins for his quick and decisive handling of the situation.

That night at dinner, the family rehashes the eventful day. During the course of the lively conversation, Carl asked this question: "How effective do you think our assignments were in helping us solve this problem?"

Overall, the family agreed that the options they selected were effective in getting the situation under control and resolved. In retrospect, however, Sam felt that he should have talked to one of his teachers, the dean, or the principal immediately following Markus's threat. Speaking supportively, Tina offered, "You learned a valuable lesson. Remember: Feedback, never failure. Now you will know what to do should something like this ever happen again. And let's hope that it doesn't!"

Following the family's assessment of their problem-solving approach, Carl and Tina once again encourage their sons to use D-BEST to find solutions to their problems and to come to them for help when they are having difficulty solving more serious or complicated problems like the one Sam had with Markus.

> Carl: No matter what, make sure you tell us if someone has threatened to hurt you. Okay?
>
> (Jimmy and Sam both enthusiastically agree.)
>
> Sam: I'm glad I told you about my problem because at first I didn't know what to do. But once I talked about it and you showed me how to solve it with D-BEST, I learned that you can find a solution if you ask for help, think about it, and go step by step. Now that I know there is a way to solve problems, I will try to do it by myself. But if I ever have a problem like this again, or one I can't solve, I will definitely let you know so you can help me find a solution. I've learned my lesson!
>
> Jimmy: Hey don't forget about me! We never got to any of my problems.
>
> (In unison, the family lets out a chuckle of relief).

Tina: I know. We will help you solve them during our next
Family Time.

Jimmy: Good. I guarantee they won't be anything like this
last one!

By teaching children how to solve problems with D-BEST, you
are equipping them with a life long skill for managing life toward hopeful
results. When demand exceeds resources, kids will know how to find the
additional resources they need to resolve the problem. And each time
they do this, they will become that much more capable of handling future
challenges. Eventually they will have the confidence and skills to find
what they need to promote the life they want. Hopelessness doesn't stand
a chance!

Now, let's see how D-BEST is used by a father with his five year-
old daughter. Tom is working in the yard as his young daughter Angela
plays across the street with her neighbor friend, Julie. Tom hears a tearful
wail and looks up to see Angela running to him with a broken doll in her
hand. Seeing she is distraught, he kneels down to give her a hug and ask
her what is going on:

Tom: Angela, what's wrong? Why are you crying?

Angela: (sobbing) Julie hurt my doll!

Tom: (looking at the doll with a missing leg) It does look like
she was treated roughly. (Hugs Angela) I know you are upset,
honey, but I need you to stop crying first, and then Daddy
can help you. (Tom waits a few minutes while Angela calms
down and wipes Angela's face off).

APPLYING D-BEST TO ANGELA'S PROBLEM

*D = DEFINE the problem: who, what, when, where, why (five Ws)
and how:*

Tom sees that Angela is facing a problem she cannot cope with alone at her age. He will ask her simple questions to get more information about how the doll was damaged.

> Tom: Okay, Angela, I'm going to ask you a few questions so I can learn what happened. Can you tell me when and where Julie hurt the doll?
>
> Angela: We were in Julie's bedroom playing. That's when she took it from me!
>
> Tom: How did the doll get hurt?
>
> Angela: Julie said, "Let me play with her." I said, "No, she's mine, I don't want to share." I was holding it and she tried to take it. She pulled and yelled and this *(pointing to piece missing from doll)* is what she did.

B = BRAINSTORM options to solve the problem:

Now that Tom has heard what occurred to Angela and her doll, he will walk Angela through the process of problem-solving. Because Angela may not be able to see many possible solutions to the problem, Tom will offer and present ideas as well.

> Tom: I can see that one of your dolls legs is broken off and that you are upset. Together, we're going to think of ways to help you, Julie and your doll. I want you to help me think of three things we can do so this does not happen again, okay? *(Angela nods)* I'll go first. One thing I can do to help is to glue the doll's leg back on. She won't be as strong as she was before though, so you will have to be very careful when you play with her. What are some other things you can do?
>
> Angela: Never play with Julie again!
>
> Tom: You and Julie have lots of fun together. Don't you think you would be sad if you never played with her again?

Angela: *(hesitating)* Well, I could get a new doll.

Tom: You did a good job thinking of those ideas. Now, do you remember what all three of our ideas were?

Angela: Fix the doll, don't play with Julie, and get another doll.

Tom: Good memory! Now, I will help you evaluate each of those three ideas and you tell me which one is best.

Now, Tom helps Angela move to the third stage of the D-BEST process—Evaluate.

E = EVALUATE the options until a potential solution is found:

In this stage, Tom will evaluate each of their brainstormed options to determine which ones will be the most effective in helping solve Angela's problem. Below is a summary of what Tom determined for each option:

• *Tom will glue the doll's leg back on*

Tom is willing to reapply the doll's leg but explains to Angela that the doll could easily break in the same place again.

• *Angela will never play with Julie again.*

Julie and Angela spend a great deal of time together, and Tom knows that his daughter will miss her company after Angela forgets about the doll incident. Tom explains to his daughter that accidents do happen, and although Julie shouldn't have grabbed and pulled the doll so hard, Angela should also be willing to share her toys when she is playing with friends. If she does not choose to share, then she should not take her toys over to Julie's house with her.

• *Angela gets a new doll.*

Tom would buy Angela a comparable doll to replace the one that was broken. Tom is willing to do this, but if rough play becomes a pattern with Julie and Angela, then he will reevaluate and determine if he needs to bring the behavior to the attention of Julie's parents.

S = SELECT the best options.

Tom: Now that we have evaluated our options, it is time to *select* the best one. Which one do you think is best?

Angela: I want a new doll!

Tom: I think that in this case, this is the best solution for now. We can look for a doll together at the store next time we go. I want you to forgive Julie for hurting your doll and promise me that you will let Julie play with your new doll. If you don't share, then you won't have many friends. Will you share your new doll with Julie?

Angela: Yes, but not if she's pulling.

Tom: If Julie hurts your doll again, I will talk to her parents, but I think this time it was an accident where you were both at fault. Now, how about you go back in the house and get your hands and face washed for dinner?

Angela: *(Walking away with her doll)* Dinner. I'm hungry!

T = TEST the options to determine if they solve the problem:

The next weekend, Tom allows Angela to choose a comparably priced doll from the store. When Julie comes over to play, Tom sits down with the two girls and talks about the importance of sharing. He begins by talking to Julie.

Tom: *(showing Julie the new doll)* Julie, we just bought this doll for Angela, so she is very special to her, and we do not want her to get hurt. This means that we do not pull or hit the doll or do anything to damage it. Do you think you can play nicely with the doll?

Julie: Yes.

Tom: *(turning to his daughter)* Angela, will you share the doll with Julie while she plays with you today?

Angela: Yes, Daddy.

Tom goes back to his chores around the house but keeps an open ear for any further trouble. After Julie returns home without any further incident, he is satisfied that the option tested well.

FIND ASSIGNMENTS

FIND Assignment 1: *Apply the D-Best Method to your own problems.*

Go back to the problem you identified in FIND Strategy 1. On a piece of paper, go through the five steps of D-BEST to decide how to solve the problem. Married couples might want to do this together for added brainstorming input. Try the method on a couple more problems so that you become familiar with it.

Remember, if you have a serious problem that you can't solve on your own—drugs, alcohol, gambling, depression, anger or whatever—find and ask for help you need to get back in control. (See the resource list at the end of the chapter.) Remember this sobering truth: violence, suicide, and drugs destroy hope. Destroy them before they destroy your family.

FIND Assignment 2: *Plan how you will teach D-BEST during Hopeful Hour.*

Take note of the ages and needs of your children. Brainstorm what teaching methods might be most effective to help them understand the D-BEST concept. For instance, you might make some visual aids on a set of large index cards or small posters. You might plan to go into the session with some examples already selected to talk about while you introduce the method. Perhaps your family jointly faces a problem that affects all of you. This might relate to a family pet, transportation issue, family schedule, chores or anything that affects the entire family. Solving this problem together could be a good teaching tool to introduce the method. Have a plan for approaching this important time together and remind yourself to keep your cool if something comes up that alarms you.

HOPEFUL HOUR PLANNING PAGE

Write in your own words the main substance of Principle 5: FIND:

```
┌──────────────────────────────────────────────────┐
│                                                    │
│   _____   │
│                                                    │
│   _____   │
│                                                    │
│   _____   │
│                                                    │
└──────────────────────────────────────────────────┘
```

Plan how many Hopeful Hours you think you'll need to devote to this principle. List the dates you will have these Hopeful Hours. Jot down a key activity you will use in each Hopeful Hour to engage your children in learning the principle. Your activities may be suggestions you find in the chapter or adaptations you know your child will enjoy. Make sure your plan includes all the key strategies of the principle. Continue on an additional sheet of paper if necessary.

	Date	Strategy	Key Activity

CHAPTER 9

Principle 6:
UNDERSTAND (Part 1)

OBJECTIVE 6A: Learn to ask questions and listen to your child.

Parent: How can I understand my child?

Wise man: You must do two things.

Parent: What two things?

Wise man: You are doing one of them right now.

Parent: What am I doing?

Wise man: You are asking me a question.

Parent: And what is the other thing?

Wise man: You are doing it right now.

Parent: What am I doing?

Wise man: You are listening to my answer.

Parent: That's it?

Wise man: Yes. Ask, then listen, and you will understand your child.

The easiest way to understand kids, or anyone else for that matter, is to ask questions, then listen to their answers. When we do this with openness and caring, hopefulness thrives. Unfortunately, much too often we fail to follow this simple approach because we are too busy doing something else or in too much of a hurry to be somewhere else. Consequently, we talk *at* rather than *with* our children. Following our example, our kids do the same. The result? Misunderstandings and missed opportunities to make a difference.

To reverse this discouraging trend, Principle 6: UNDERSTAND will show you how to get back to the basics of effective communication: asking questions and listening to the answers. In UNDERSTAND Part 1, we'll focus on strategies for simply asking and listening. In UNDERSTAND Part 2 (Chapter Ten), we'll look specifically at responding to what you hear by helping your child replace self-talk that brings hope down with self-talk that builds hope up.

UNDERSTAND STRATEGIES

UNDERSTAND Strategy 1. Show your child that you care by asking questions based on the five Ws and How: *Who, What, When, Where, Why, and How*

A popular campaign says Asking Saves Kids (ASK). The campaign is based on the idea that if parents ask if neighbors have guns in the home before sending their kids over to play, fewer children will be lost to the senseless destruction of playing with guns. Asking kids questions can have similar benefits. By asking your children questions, you could literally save their lives and protect them from the deadly effects common to violence, suicide, drugs and bad choices.

As a parent, you not only have the right to ask your child questions you have the responsibility for asking questions as a way to be involved in your child's life and more important, to keep him or her out of harm's way and headed in the right direction. Moreover, asking questions is not an invasion of privacy. Rather, it is a process of normalcy because open communication requires parents and their kids to ask each other questions to stay abreast of changes, to determine needs, and to keep a pulse on what is going on in one another's lives and in the family.

Ultimately, asking questions gives you the opportunity to prove to your kids that you are interested in who they are becoming and what is happening in their lives. And, equally as important, it reserves you an opportunity to help when they are in the midst of a crisis and face hard choices. The easiest way to accomplish this is to ask questions based on the familiar five *Ws* and *How*. Here are some examples:

- Who are you going out with tonight?
- Who will be at the party tonight?
- What is the address of the party?
- What can you tell me about this beer can I found in the back of your car?
- When does the party end?
- When will you call me this evening?
- Where are you going this evening?
- Where is your friend's house?
- Why did you choose this movie?
- Why are you so tired today?
- How did you get that cut on your knuckle?
- How do you get to your friend's house?

Obviously, there are an infinite number of questions you could ask about what is going on in a child's life. Hence, circumstances will dictate the type of question you will need to ask. The most important thing, though, is that you do it. Ask the question. As long as you respect your child by valuing individuality and ideas, you should experience little resistance. If, however, you do experience some resistance, let your child know that you ask questions because you have a responsibility to keep him safe. Also, you care about *who* he is becoming, *what* is important, *why* your child views things a particular way, *where* life is taking your child, *when* he wants to get there, and *how* he plans to get there. But mostly, make sure your child knows that you ask questions out of love. That's the bottom line. Thus, do whatever it takes to maintain open communication with your son or daughter by asking questions.

The next strategy will show you what to do once you've asked a question or when your child wants to talk with you.

UNDERSTAND Strategy 2: *Listen to your child and you will understand.*

The key to understanding your child is to *listen*—not merely hearing words, but truly listening. Unfortunately, because of the hustle-bustle way in which we conduct our lives, little time is invested in meaning-fully communicating with others, let alone our kids. What follows is an example of what commonly happens between a parent and a child when the parent fails to make an investment in *listening* to what her child is really saying. Sadly, it is more often the rule than the exception. Pay attention to how the parent, by not listening, is talking *at* rather than *with* her child.

A mother is busy reconciling her checkbook and going over the previous month's bills as her twelve-year-old daughter returns from soccer practice.

> Daughter: *(enters the kitchen where her mother is working on her checkbook)* Hey, Mom, what's up?
> Mom: *(head down)* Trying to figure out where all of our money is going. *(continues working calculator)* How was practice?
> Daughter: *(hesitating)* Practice went well, but there was this weird-looking guy that kept hanging around the soccer

field. He kept waving at me. He gave me the creeps.

Mom: *(writing in checkbook)* Did you score any goals?

Daughter: *(frustrated)* No, I didn't score any goals. I was more concerned about the creepy guy who kept waving and smiling at me. I tried to ignore him, but no matter what I did, he kept trying to get my attention. I have no idea what he wanted, but I am sure it wasn't anything good.

Mom: *(looking quizzically at a bill)* Your father and I don't approve of you spending time with boys unless we know about it first. You should be practicing, not flirting.

Daughter: *(agitated)* I wasn't flirting. That's not what was going on at all. You have no clue what I am talking about! *(grabs her stuff and stomps toward the stairs)*

Mom: *(startled)* What's with the attitude? Did you hear me?

Daughter: Yeah, I heard you. I wish you would do the same. You never listen to me! *(slams door)*

What happened? This mother completely misunderstood and missed an opportunity for open communication with her daughter at an important time. This misunderstanding could have tragic results. And each time this happens, her daughter will be less and less likely to tell her mother about other potentially harmful situations. The simple truth is, this whole mess could have been easily averted and resolved had the mother practiced good listening skills. To prevent this from happening to you with your son or daughter, follow these steps to effective listening.

First, stop doing whatever you are doing and listen. You can't do two things at the same time and expect to do either one well. If you are busy doing something when your child wants to talk, ask her this question: "Is it important that we speak right now, or can this wait until I am finished?" Remember, you learned in Principle 2: OPEN that you should automatically stop doing whatever you are doing and listen when your son or daughter says, "I need you." Now that you have stopped what you are doing, focus on your child. S–L–O–W down. Take in a few relaxing breaths and pay attention to what is really going on and being said. Nothing is more important than what your child has to say at this important moment—nothing. Make this time to listen your priority. Everything else can wait.

Next, empathize with your child by making your best effort to genuinely feel what he or she is communicating to you. Just as important, show that what your child has to say is important to you by constantly validating and encouraging. You can easily accomplish this through good eye contact and by nodding your head affirmatively while your child speaks. And finally, as a general rule, listen twice as much as you talk. Remember, you have two ears and one mouth. The following approach to effective listening is summarized by using the word LISTEN as our guide:

> L = Listen twice as much as you talk: Two ears, one mouth
>
> I = Invest all of yourself in listening to your child: physically, emotionally and mentally.
>
> S = Stop doing whatever you are doing and listen to your child. Do one thing well—LISTEN.
>
> T = Take time to listen. The other stuff can wait.
>
> E = Empathize with your child by trying to feel what she feels.
>
> N = Nothing is more important than listening to your child when she needs you—nothing!

Now it's time to put your new asking-and-listening skills to work with your family.

AT MY HOUSE

> **Think honestly about a recent situation where you were not listening carefully as your child spoke to you. Describe the situation, then say what you could have done to be a better listener. If appropriate, plan to apologize to your child for not listening better.**
>
> _____
>
> _____
>
> _____
>
> _____
>
> _____
>
> _____

UNDERSTAND Strategy 3: *Ask your child a positive question every day.*

Undoubtedly you've heard the age-old belief that "an apple a day keeps the doctor away." Well, with hopefulness in mind, you will now come to understand this basic truth: "A positive question a day helps keep hopelessness away."

This is true because every time you ask your child a question, you are demonstrating that you care about who he is becoming, what he is doing, when he is doing it, where he is doing it, why he is doing it and how he is doing it. Sure, he may become a little perturbed now and then when you ask a question; that's normal, but the cost is well worth the benefit—a Hopeful Kid. Think of it this way: The opposite of asking is apathy. Put into a sentence, if you don't ask your child questions, you are proving that you don't care about what is happening in his life. Keep this in mind the next time you feel it's not worth the effort because your child may resist you once in awhile. You will soon find out that the more consistent you are in asking a question each and every day, the more comfortable he will become in answering your question. In fact, he will begin to look forward to your daily inquiry about his ever-changing life. And don't be surprised when one day these positive questions will lead to increased openness and spontaneous revelations about other areas of his life.

It is very simple to implement this strategy. First, think of a positive question you want to ask your child each day. It doesn't have to be profound. In fact, simple is best. Try to keep the question focused on everyday situations relevant to his present-day life and activities. Here are some examples:

- What did you do after school today?
- Where are you going on your next field trip?
- What was the best part of your day?
- When are you planning your next sleepover?
- How were things at school/work today?
- What was your most memorable event today?
- Who did you hang out with today?
- What are your plans for this weekend?

AT MY HOUSE

Add your own examples of positive questions that relate particularly to your child and his or her interests.

_____

_____

_____

_____

Once you've determined the question you want to ask, it is important that you ask the question at about the same time every day. I recommend that you do this at the end of the day: after school, before dinner, during dinner, after dinner, etc. Also, make a conscious effort to *listen* once you've asked the question. Nothing is more annoying to a child than a parent who asks a question but doesn't listen to the answer. And finally, don't have any expectations about how your child should respond. Let him or her determine the quality and volume of the answer based on experiences during the day. Most of the time you will receive a positive response and, less often, a one-word or two-word answer. It doesn't matter, since the main point you are making when you ask a question is that you are interested in, value, and, most important, love your child. As you do this consistently, day in and day out, a natural flow will emerge, and the conversation will become more fluid, more open, and more spontaneous. Remember, it all begins with a question: Ask!

UNDERSTAND Strategy 4: *Learn to better understand your child by playing The Asking-and-Listening Game.*

Play this game during your family's Hopeful Hour. The objective here is to better understand one another by asking some fun, challenging and serious questions.

Begin by having each person in the group list three to five questions that he or she wants to ask one or more family members in the group. The basic rule applied to each question is this: It can be about anything as long as it does not criticize, degrade or purposely embarrass the person being asked the question. In all cases, however, answers must be open and honest. And parents, be prepared for your son or daughter to ask you questions that will challenge your comfort zone. When this happens, do your best at being an example of open communication because your child will follow your behavior. Remember, behavior speaks louder than words. If you are uncomfortable, say so, and then answer the question the best you can. If the question is inappropriate, explain why it is inappropriate. Ask why your son or daughter wants to ask you this question, then use this opportunity to demonstrate a more respectful way of asking the question. Be mindful, however, that whenever you establish a boundary about asking a question, you are clearly communicating that your child has the same right. Therefore, choose your limits carefully because it is difficult to have open, no-limit communication if you have limits.

By opening up your boundaries you are challenging your child to do the same. And each time you show a willingness to be open even when you are uncomfortable, your child will be more likely to follow your example. Eventually, he or she will transfer lessons from this game—trust, openness, and confidence—to everyday reality. This will pay off big time when your child is embroiled in a difficult situation and is looking for input before making a crucial decision. Following your example of openness, he or she will surely give you an opportunity to help.

Bottom line: open up!

HOPEFUL HOUR TIP

 You can play The Asking-and-Listening Game with easy questions, then proceed to more challenging and serious questions later on. For example, your first question might be: "If you could be an animal (car, musical instrument, food, etc.), what would you be and why?" And later on, something like this: "What color best describes your mood?" Then you might ask: "What would you do if someone offered you drugs?" or "What would you do if one of your friends wanted to show you a gun he'd brought to school?" or "What would you do if one of your friends told he wanted to hurt someone?" You get the idea. Take this gradual, staircase approach to asking questions and you will soon notice that as the trust and comfort level increases, so too will the level of openness.

Let's go over the actual process of how the game is played. Allow five to ten minutes for individuals to compose their respective list of questions (three to five each). Next, let someone volunteer to ask the first question, then take turns until all the questions are asked or until time runs out. If you run out of time before you finish all the questions, let kids know when you'll play again so they don't feel ignored or left out.

As the question-and-answer sequence is going on, pay attention to group dynamics. That is, look for positive and negative reactions both verbally and non-verbally. Constantly encourage and reinforce curiosity, directness, honesty, and openness. If, however, someone becomes uncomfortable, ask that person if he or she wants to continue or come back to the question later. In the event someone becomes upset, encourage him to take a break until he is ready to answer the question or discuss his feelings at a later date. (Refer to Take Ten and Think–Choose–Act under Principle 2: OPEN for help in these situations.) Remember, though, this is a game! Getting upset and angry should be the exception rather than the norm. Thus, do everything you can to have fun, learn something new about one another, and enjoy this opportunity to be together as a family. Finally, keep this thought paramount as you play this game: The only wrong question is the one you don't ask. It could make the difference between a good choice or a bad choice, purpose or confusion, hope or despair, life or death. Remember, ASK Asking Saves Kids—your kids.

The Center for Mental Health Services has created a series of conversation-starters to encourage family interaction by talking and listening. It is appropriately titled *Make Time to Listen—Take Time to Talk*. The questions range from easy to challenging and are well-suited for children of all ages. It is a great companion to this principle in helping you hone your skills in understanding your son or daughter. Better yet, it is absolutely free! You can get it by calling (800) 789-2647 and following the recorded directions or visiting www.mentalhealth.org and printing the material right from the site. Do yourself a big favor and get this awesome resource as soon as possible. You'll be glad you did.

UNDERSTAND ASSIGNMENTS PART 1

UNDERSTAND Assignment 1: *Remember events from your childhood.*

This assignment will require you to get inside that time machine you keep parked in your mind and return to that time and place when you were your child's age or thereabouts. Try to recall some events, good and bad, that stand out in your mind's eye. No rush, just let it happen as it happens. Next, identify those situations that generate the most thinking and feeling. Then, isolate three positive and three negative events. Spend some time re-experiencing these awesome and awkward moments. Now, imagine some of the questions you wished your parents had asked you to better understand what was going on in your life at that time.

When you have finished reminiscing, write down the top three questions you would have wanted your parents to ask you for both of the positive and negative events:

Positive Event Questions:

1. _____

_____

2. _____

_____

3. _____

_____

Negative Event Questions:

1. _____

_____

2. _____

_____

3. _____

_____

UNDERSTAND Assignment 2: *Determine the questions to ask your children.*

Look at the questions you documented above. Now determine if these are the type of questions your child would want you to ask given your child's age, maturity and experience. Circle these questions. Next, rewrite them in a way that your child would understand.

Positive Event Questions:

1. _____

_____

2. _____

_____

3. _____

_____

Negative Event Questions:

1. _____

_____

2. _____

_____

3. _____

_____

UNDERSTAND Assignment 3: *Ask your child key questions—and listen.*

Create an opportunity to make a difference in your child's life by asking each of these questions and listening to the answers. Remember what the wise man said: "Ask, then listen, and you will understand your child." It all begins with the first question: Ask!

HOPEFUL HOUR PLANNING PAGE

Write in your own words the main substance of Principle 6: UNDERSTAND (Part 1):

Plan how many Hopeful Hours you think you'll need to devote to this principle. List the dates you will have these Hopeful Hours. Jot down a key activity you will use in each Hopeful Hour to engage your children in learning the principle. Your activities may be suggestions you find in the chapter or adaptations you know your child will enjoy. Make sure your plan includes all the key strategies of the principle. Continue on an additional sheet of paper if necessary.

Date	Strategy	Key Activity

CHAPTER 10

Principle 6: UNDERSTAND (Part 2)

OBJECTIVE 6B: Teach your child to recognize hope-suckers and hope-creators.

Understanding your child begins with asking questions and listening to the answers—really listening. But what do you do with what you hear? We might not like to admit we are "hearing voices," but we all have inner scripts that remind us what others believe about us or what we believe about ourselves. This self-talk can be negative or positive. It can drain the hope out of us, or it can fill us with hope. We all engage in activities or relationships that drain us or enliven us.

It's your job as parents to understand what makes your kids tick. It's your job as parents to make sure your kids' self-talk is positive and hopeful. It's your job to make sure activities and relationships are healthy and empowering, not draining and destructive. It's your job to make sure your kids know the difference between the things that drain hope away and the things that make hope flow in. It's your job to act on what you hear your kids say.

The strategies in this chapter will help you take what you learn about your kids and use it to give them a new skill for a lifetime.

UNDERSTAND STRATEGIES (PART 2)

UNDERSTAND Strategy 5: *Identify your child's hope-suckers and hope-creators.*

The labels I suggest are pretty clear. They mean what they imply. Hope-suckers are those people, activities, and things that literally suck the hope out of your child. Conversely, hope-creators are people, activities and things that inspire and sustain hope in your son or daughter. Hope-suckers can be obvious—drugs and violent peers—or obscure and less tangible yet equally as destructive: negative self-talk, violent music, and negative role models. Similarly, hope-creators can be obvious—goals and positive peers—or less obvious yet equally as powerful in instilling hope in your son or daughter: hopeful self-talk, inspiring books, and positive role models. That said, your objective in this strategy is to systematically replace your son or daughter's hope-suckers with hope-creators. You will accomplish this life-saving goal by using your asking-and-listening skills. Do this with great attention, patience, and compassion and you will come to understand exactly those elements that are crushing or cultivating hope in your child's life.

Below is a brief list of hope-suckers and hope-creators. Take notice that for every *sucker* there is a *creator*. Use the list as a general guide to identify people, activities and things that encourage or discourage hope in your child. Be sure to highlight those areas that are having the greatest influence on your child's development or decline.

Please note this is a general list and may or may not apply to your child. You are the judge of that based on your knowledge of your kid.

HOPE-SUCKERS	HOPE-CREATORS
Younger Children	**Younger Children**
• Kids who hit other kids. • Kids who tease and frequently call others names and use bad language. • Kids who are disorderly and out of control. • Kids who steal.	• Kids who respect physical boundaries. • Kids who compliment and have self-control in their words. • Kids with good manners. • Kids who respect others property.
Pre-teens and Teens	**Pre-teens and Teens**
• Violent/angry or very negative peers. • Peers who use drugs and/or alcohol. • Peers who are in a gang. • Peers who focus on the dark side of life. • Role models who foster hopelessness: Satanic heavy-metal bands, violent rap singers, drug-addicted movie stars, egotistical athletes.	• Peers who have positive attitudes and social skills. • Drug and alcohol-free peers involved in positive activities. • Peers who belong to positive groups. • Peers who are active in their community, church, sports, volunteer work, employment. • Peers who make an effort to overcome adversity. • Role models who foster hopefulness: socially conscious musical groups, community-minded movie stars and athletes.
Activities	**Activities**
• Listening to music that reinforces hopeless themes: violence, suicide, drugs, hate • Playing violent video or computer games. • Watching movies or TV shows that focus on violence, drugs, suicide, sex. • Reading material that reinforces hopeless ideas: death, destruction, despair, drugs, deviance, delinquency. • Inactivity: sitting around doing nothing. • Social gatherings that encourage drug or alcohol use or deviance.	• Listening to music with hopeful themes: love, truth, trust, commitment, courage. • Playing games that enhance learning and confidence. • Watching movies that focus on hopefulness: courage, overcoming adversity, love, challenge. • Reading material that promotes hope: inspirational biographies, self-help, skill-development, educational, spirituality. • Activity: sports, school clubs, church. • Social gatherings that promote a drug-free, alcohol-free environment and positive interaction.

Things	Things
• Any clothes, jewelry, or accessories that inspire hopelessness: cults, gangs, drugs, violence, prejudice, hate.	• Any clothes, jewelry, or accessories that inspire hopefulness: "I can create the life I want through positive choices and goals."

As a parent, you well know that this list only scratches the surface of the great many elements that can inspire or frustrate hope in a young person. Accordingly, use it as a reference point as you work with your child to identify and replace the suckers with creators.

AT MY HOUSE

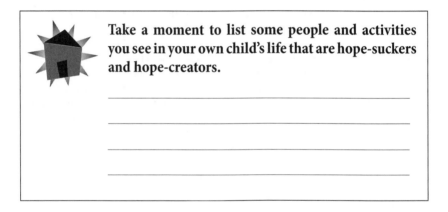

Take a moment to list some people and activities you see in your own child's life that are hope-suckers and hope-creators.

_____

_____

_____

_____

Now, let's go over how you will actually go about replacing hope-suckers with hope-creators, step by step, with your son or daughter.

To begin, tell your child that you want to work together on creating more hope in your child's life. Say that you will do this by helping to replace those things that discourage hope—hope-suckers— with things that encourage hope—hope-creators. Next, have your child draw a vertical line down the middle of a piece of paper in the Hopeful Kid's Notebook. On the top left side of the paper, write "Hope Suckers" and on the top right side write "Hope Creators." Now have your child list the top five people, peers, activities and things that are causing the greatest level of hopelessness. Be aware that the list may be very short, one or two items, or longer, five to ten items, depending on what is going on in your kid's life. The length doesn't matter. What really matters is understanding exactly what is sucking the hope out of your kid so you can help replace those things with hope-creators. Allow as much time as your child needs to complete the list. Normally, it will take between ten and thirty minutes to develop.

UNDERSTAND Strategy 6: *Teach the Hope Testing technique.*

I want to introduce you to a very simple yet highly effective method for teaching your child how to distinguish hope-suckers from hope-creators. I call it Hope Testing. Moreover, it is one of the best ways to teach your child how to independently evaluate options. And as you recall from the Principle 3: PURPOSE, the skill of independent evaluation will help your youngster make more responsible and purposeful decisions. Here is how it works. When your child's list of hope-suckers is complete, engage him in the process of Hope Testing by asking how each of these hope-suckers relates to the life your child wants with questions like these.

> How does this crush hope in your life?
> How does this prevent you from achieving your goals?
> How does this prevent you from becoming a Hopeful Kid?
> Do you understand how this crushes hope in your life?
> Do you understand how this is causing you to feel so bad?
> What can you do to feel better?

It is crucial that you and your child understand how each of these people, activities, and things causes hopelessness. This conscious understanding will get your child on track, or back on track, to being a Hopeful Kid. Furthermore, it will show the value of being involved with peers and activities that are in line with positive goals. Finally, and just as important, it will teach how to independently identify and avoid other hope-suckers down the road. Accordingly, take as much time as you need to complete this exercise.

Once you are finished Hope Testing, you are ready for the second part of this strategy: Replace the hope-suckers with hope-creators. On the opposite side of the paper and directly across from each hope-sucker, challenge your child to identify those people, activities, and things that *create* hope with these inspiring requests:

- Show me how you can replace this hope-sucker with a hope-creator.
- What can you do differently that will help you create the life you want?
- What can you do instead that will help you achieve your goals?
- How does this create hope in your life?
- Explain how you can get back on target with your goal.

Try these questions or come up with other questions that fit your youngster's personality, hopeful passion and focus. Again, invest as much time as you need to ensure that your kid understands the need to replace all of the hope-suckers with hope-creators and how to do it.

Hopeful Hour Tip

 You can bolster kids' confidence and desire to stick with the plan through goal-setting, role-playing, ongoing progress reports, as well as daily asking-and-listening interactions. And, of course, constantly remind your child of your belief in his or her ability to make positive choices that lead to positive outcomes. In the end, your well-tuned ability to understand your kid will lead you to successfully teach how to find and attract those people, activities and things that create hope today, tomorrow, and for the rest of his or her life.

Hope Testing is the most effective way to get your child back on the hopeful journey when her behavior causes her to stray. Moreover, it is one of the best strategies to teach your child how to independently evaluate options when you can't be there. A child who learns how to do this independently will have developed the personal power to create the life he or she wants for a lifetime.

Understand Strategy 7: *Replace negative self-talk with hopeful talk.*

Self-talk is what we say to ourselves either out loud or internally. When self-talk is positive, it is one of the most powerful forces for creating hope. This is called Hopeful Talk. On the other hand, when self-talk is negative, it is one of the most destructive forces in crushing hope. This is Hopeless Talk. Here are some examples of both:

Hopeful Talk	Hopeless Talk
I know how to make positive choices.	I can't do anything right.
I want to achieve my goals.	My life is going nowhere.
I can create the life I want.	I have nothing to look forward to.
I am smart.	I am stupid.
I get along well with others.	No one likes me.
I can handle this problem.	Nothing works out for me.
I am confident about my abilities.	I am useless.
I like my life.	I hate my life.
I am hopeful.	I am hopeless.

Given this, it is crucial that you pay attention to what your child says on a daily basis. Promote Hopeful Talk by making great efforts at reinforcing it, rewarding it, and modeling it. (This is a perfect opportunity to be a Hopeful Example for your kid.) Make sure your children know you care enough to pay attention to how they talk to themselves and to others. In those instances when you hear Hopeless Talk (hope-suckers), immediately work with your youngster to replace it with Hopeful Talk (hope-creators). And as you already know, use Hope Testing to accomplish this objective by testing negative, hopeless verbalizations against the Hopeful Motto and Purpose. To accomplish this, try this pair of hope-provoking questions:

- How does that kind of negative talk help you to achieve your goals?
- What can you say instead that will help you get what you want out of life?

Get kids to the point where they can do this on their own, and they will be well on the way to engaging themselves, as well as others, in more Hopeful Talk and creating the life they want through positive choices and goals. Hopeful Kids talk hopefully.

Let's put these strategies to work with the Wilson family.

THE WILSON FAMILY TAKES TIME TO UNDERSTAND

Let's drop in again on the Wilson family, whom we met in Principle 1: HOUR and Principle 5: FIND. Now let's see how Tina Wilson uses her understanding skills to help her nine-year-old son, Jimmy, handle a situation involving cigarettes. Keep in mind that the following events could take place any time, any place, anywhere, and with any kid—your kid. Therefore, try to imagine how you would handle a similar situation, regardless of the type of drug—nicotine, marijuana, cocaine, crank, heroin, ecstasy, crystal-meth, PCP, crack—with your son or daughter using the strategies you learned here. And by the way, if you don't recognize any of the aforementioned drugs, how will you recognize them when your child asks you about them? You won't! Consequently, do everything you can to learn about the numerous drugs that are on the streets before they end up in your child. Bottom line: The more you *understand*, the more you can help.

Here is the scene: It is a Thursday afternoon and Tina is busy studying for her midterm for her psychology class. Her husband, Carl, is still at work, and her two sons, Jimmy and Sam, age eleven, are about to return from basketball practice. Her plan is to have the boys complete their homework and chores, then watch television or play quietly. Additionally, Carl has agreed to pitch in by cooking dinner when he gets home. If everything goes as planned, she will gain two additional hours of study time before dinner is ready. She is really counting on all of this working out because this may be one of the last opportunities she will have to study before her exam on Monday. What she doesn't know, however, is that her understanding skills are about to be put to the test. Pay attention to how the next thirty minutes will change a son, a mother, and a family forever.

Opportunity knocks: As expected, Jimmy and Sam return from practice on time. Sam hurries past Tina as he makes his way to his bedroom. Tina reminds him to complete his homework and chores by dinner. Jimmy, on the other hand, sits down at the dinner table where Tina is studying.

> Jimmy: *(seems tense)* What are you doing?
> Tina: *(looks up)* Studying for my big test on Monday.
> Jimmy: Oh. *(breathes an audible sigh)*

Reading his body language and tone, Tina knows something is bothering Jimmy, but she is ambivalent about asking him about it because she really needs to get ready for her midterm. She also knows that this may be her only opportunity to influence Jimmy if there are difficult decisions to be made. Realizing this possibility, Tina places a marker in her book and closes it. She looks directly at Jimmy.

> Tina: Is something bothering you?
> Jimmy: *(pauses slightly)* Sort of.
> Tina: Is there anything you want to talk with me about? Anything at all?

Jimmy: *(fidgets in chair)* Maybe. But you're pretty busy. I can talk with you later.

Tina: *(visibly pushes book aside and leans toward Jimmy)* Nothing is more important to me than what you want to talk about right now—nothing. I'll find time to study later. So let's talk about whatever is on your mind.

Jimmy: *(relieved)* All right. I do need to ask you about something that happened today, but you have to promise not to get mad.

Tina: Jimmy, I can't promise I won't get upset until I know what you want to talk about. However, I promise I will never get mad at you for talking with my about something that's bothering you. No matter what! Do you understand?

Jimmy: Yeah. Okay. Here's what I need to talk about. This guy offered me a cigarette. He said it would make me feel really cool without hurting me. Is that true?

Tina: He did what?

Tina caught herself from losing control. She tried to regain her composure by using Take Ten. During this time-out, she took in some deep breaths and let them out slowly. Jimmy was wide-eyed and timid.

Jimmy: Mom, are you getting mad?

Tina: Yes, but give me a minute to regroup.

Jimmy: Okay.

Tina is deeply disturbed by what her nine-year-old son is asking her. Nonetheless, she knows that whatever she says next will have a lasting impact on her son's present and future decisions to use, or not to use, not only cigarettes, but other things as well, such as alcohol or drugs. Speaking assertively, she begins this way:

Tina: Jimmy, the nicotine and tobacco in cigarettes are extremely dangerous and addictive. It may make you feel good for a short time, but ultimately it will cause you a lifetime of pain. And just like any other addictive, its positive effects are short lived, and eventually it will have just the opposite effect. It will cause you to feel bad—bad about life and bad about yourself. Do you understand what I am saying to you?

Jimmy: (seems confused) Yeah, but this guy told me that everyone does it.

Tina: I don't use it, and neither does your father or brother. And I don't know anyone else who smokes. The bottom line is this: tobacco and addictive drugs harm you physically and can lead to a life of hopelessness. So the best way to not get addicted is to never start taking them in the first place! That is why we are always telling you, "Hope not dope."

Tina gives Jimmy some time to comprehend what she just said, then asks.

Tina: Do you remember us telling you not to take anything unless it comes from your doctor or from us?

Jimmy: (looking at his mother) Yeah, I remember. That's why I am talking to you about this right now, because I don't know what to do.

Tina: First of all, you are doing the right thing by coming to me about this.

Jimmy: I know. I was a little nervous at first, but now I know it was the right thing to do.

Tina: (squeezes his hand) Who is the guy that offered you the cigarette?

Jimmy: (hesitates) Do you really need to know his name?

Tina: Absolutely. I can't help you if I don't know who you are talking about.

Jimmy: (still sounding reluctant) His name is ... umm ... his name is ... Victor. He's fifteen. (slumps into chair)

Tina: How do you know him?

Jimmy: Well, I don't really know him because he's too old to go to my school. All I really know about him is that he's been hangin' around the school parking lot after basketball practice for the past couple weeks. And he's always nice to me.

Recognizing that Jimmy was young and impressionable, she pushed him to understand who Victor really is with the hard truth.

Tina: Jimmy, you need to understand that the only reason Victor is being nice to you is because he is trying to get you hooked on drugs. (waits for this to sink in) Did you know that?

Jimmy: No… I mean, I do now. But he didn't say he sold drugs, just "stuff that made people feel good."

Tina: Do you think he has your best interest in mind?

Jimmy: Probably not. He told me not to talk with you or dad about this.

Tina: What does that tell you?

Jimmy: That he is up to no good and wants me to use drugs.

Tina: Right. Jimmy, do you really believe tobacco will make you feel cool?

Jimmy: (shaking his head) No. I mean, I knew that cigarettes were bad because you and dad talked with me about this before. But Victor said that these cigarettes were "cool" and won't hurt me at all.

Tina: (emphatically) Jimmy, this guy is flat-out lying to you! He doesn't care about you one bit.

Tina compassionately challenges Jimmy by engaging him in some timely Hope Testing.

Tina: Do you see why Victor, cigarettes, and all other addictive substances are hope-suckers?

Jimmy: (thinks for a moment) I do now. I have to admit,

though, I was a little confused because I almost believed what Victor was saying even though you and dad have always told me that drugs are bad news. But now that you have told me the truth about how tobacco is a drug and that it can really hurt—or even kill you—I know why Victor and drugs are hope-suckers. They won't help me achieve my goals and be a Hopeful Kid.

Tina: Now you've got it. Jimmy, what creates hope in your life right now?

Jimmy: You mean my hope-creators? Well, most definitely my family, basketball, my goals, school, my artwork and my friends. There are probably some more things, but I can't think of them right now.

Tina: Based on what you've just said, it sounds like you understand very well the people and activities that create hope in your life. And like we have already talked about, tobacco and other addictive substances only crush hope. That is why you need to stay away from those kind of hope-suckers.

Jimmy: Absolutely! I'm so glad I had this talk with you. Thanks for listening to me Mom.

Tina: You're welcome. I will always make time to talk with you when you need me. Jimmy, I want you to know how impressed I am with your ability to make positive choices that result in positive outcomes. Talking to me about this situation was a good choice, and I hope you will always come to me when you are faced with something like this again.

Jimmy: I will, Mom. I definitely will.

Tina: Good. We all need to sit down and talk about this when your father comes home.

Jimmy: *(tentatively)* All right, but I hope he doesn't get mad.

Tina: Jimmy, what did I tell you earlier when we first sat down to talk about this and getting mad?

Jimmy: I know, you and dad will never get mad at me for telling

you about something that is bothering me, no matter what.
And nothing is more important than this right now—nothing!
Tina: That's right—nothing!

For the first time during this intense conversation, they share a moment of peace. A comfortable silence settles in as mother and son try to absorb all that has happened. Still reveling in the moment, Jimmy breaks the silence as he puts it all into perspective with this realization: "Now I know what you and dad mean when you say, 'Hope, not dope!'"

Jimmy understands!

The bottom line is that asking questions and listening to answers is the key to understanding your kid and creating an opportunity to make a difference when a difference has to be made.

UNDERSTAND ASSIGNMENTS PART 2

UNDERSTAND Assignment 4: *Identify your own hope-suckers and hope-creators.*

To identify with what your child will go through to identify hope-suckers and hope-creators, go through the exercise for yourself. Identify your own hope-suckers, the things that drain hopefulness away from you. Be an example to your children by honestly recognizing the people, activities and things that get in the way of achieving your goals and make you feel discouraged. Hope Test your answers and identify ways to turn hope-suckers into hope-creators.

UNDERSTAND Assignment 5: *Examine your family's self-talk.*

Over the period of a week, set aside a period of three days to listen carefully to the language you hear from yourself and the rest of the family. Keep a list of the self-talk you hear. Write down as much as you can remember so you can analyze it later. Some self-talk may be subtle or take the form of teasing, but it's still hope-sucking. For each child, write a brief paragraph about what you hear that child saying and what it means for teaching that child the difference between hope-suckers and hope-creators. If you catch yourself contributing to your child's hope-suckers, apologize and assure your child that you're going to be more positive. Then, during one of your Hopeful Hours, make your kid aware of what you heard her say and work with her to replace the negative self-talk with positive self-talk.

HOPEFUL HOUR PLANNING PAGE

Write in your own words the main substance of Principle 6: UNDERSTAND
(Part 2):

Date	Strategy	Key Activity

Plan how many Hopeful Hours you think you'll need to devote to this
principle. List the dates you will have these Hopeful Hours. Jot down a
key activity you will use in each Hopeful Hour to engage your children
in learning the principle. Your activities may be suggestions you find in
the chapter or adaptations you know your child will enjoy. Make sure
your plan includes all the key strategies of the principle. Continue on an
additional sheet of paper if necessary.

	Date	Strategy	Key Activity

CHAPTER ELEVEN

Principle 7: LOVE

OBJECTIVE 7: Demonstrate love to your children in specific actions.

Love.

Would anyone make a serious, credible argument that human beings don't need love? We've all heard the stories about babies lying in cribs in understaffed, overcrowded orphanages. Though their physical needs were tended to, babies who were left to lie in their cribs without affection and stimulation failed to thrive. They didn't eat well. They didn't grow. They didn't develop new physical skills. Without love none of the rest of it seemed to matter.

Without love, we do not thrive. You probably know people who have spent a lifetime making bad choices in the quest for love. They want to matter to somebody. Anybody. They live with abuse out of fear of not being lovable. They live with danger for the sake of love. They cling to all the wrong people because they just want somebody to love them, but the truth is they wouldn't recognize real love if it stared them in the face.

Make sure your child does not grow up to be one of these people. Make sure your child grows up knowing your love and never having a moment's doubt that love is a positive force, a hope-creator, an encouraging tool for making choices that move toward the bull's-eye. While we might all agree on the importance of love, we all too often fall short on demonstrating this particular conviction. These strategies will help you take practical steps to surround your child with powerful, hope-creating love. Action is the substance and proof of love. It is love made real—*doing* over *saying*. Parental love requires action because it genuinely validates your desire and commitment to help your child to create a hopeful way of life. It is your actions, not your words, that most powerfully express your love for your child. Ultimately, this is the easiest way for you to prove your love and the easiest way for your son or daughter to experience your love—*substance* over *statements*.

You picked up this book because you love your child. You've read this far because you love your child enough to want to instill hopefulness for a lifetime. Bolster everything you've learned so far about having a Hopeful Kids by making sure love is at the core of your relationship with your child. Now is the time to put your love into action by applying everything you've learned in *Hopeful Kids* to your son or daughter.

LOVE STRATEGIES

Love Strategy 1: *Tell your child "I love you" every single day.*

Chances are you do this already. If not, stop right here and figure out the next opportunity you'll have to say, "I love you" to your child. When she wakes up in the morning? When he comes home from practice? When you say goodnight? When you're making a favorite dish together? When you're playing checkers? When he comes home late for curfew?

It's simply not possible to overemphasize how important this is. Children need to hear their parents say these words in good times and bad times. Every parent-child relationship has moments of strain—perhaps entire seasons of strain. Even then, say, "I love you." Leave no room for doubt. Leave no room for a child to think you have withdrawn love because of undesirable behavior or disappointing choices. Kids need to know parents love them for who they are, not for what they do or don't do. They need to know unconditional love.

This is far from easy. Sometimes people joke that it's a good thing kids are cute because otherwise they wouldn't survive. Raising kids is a lot of work, and it's not all warm, tender moments with a fire crackling in the fireplace and the smell of fresh cookies wafting through the house. If you only say, "I love you" in picture-perfect moments, what message does that send to your kids about the moments of slamming doors and raised voices? Saying, "I love you" in good times and bad, consistently, assures kids you love them even when you don't love behavior. Eventually, they will learn to love themselves even when they fall short of their own expectations. Unconditional love gives the confidence kids need to pick themselves up, shake off the dust and get back on track. Love the child; work on the behavior.

Many families routinely say, "Love you" at the end of a phone conversation or as they go their separate ways in the morning to work and school. This is great. It keeps love front and center. But make sure it's not the unthinking equivalent of saying goodbye. Even if you do this routinely, look for other opportunities to be intentional about saying, "I love you" to your kids.

LOVE Strategy 2: *Show love in actions.*

GO BEYOND WORDS TO SURROUND YOUR CHILD WITH LOVE. ASK YOUR-SELF WHAT action says, "I love you" to your child? It might be showing up for every single soccer game. It might be the nightly snuggle-and-read routine. It might be sending your teenager text messages to find out how the big exam went. It might be stopping for ice cream on the way home from church, even if you haven't had lunch yet. A weekend camping trip, shooting hoops in the driveway before dinner, cutting short a business trip to be home for the band concert, letting your child choose the movie, flipping past the show you want to watch for the one you know your child likes—these are all small actions that communicate that your child is your number one priority and that you love enough to make sacrifices of your own time and energy.

AT MY HOUSE

> **For each child who lives in your home, write down at least one action that says love to that child and plan when you can demonstrate this action.**
>
> _____
>
> _____
>
> _____
>
> _____

LOVE Strategy 3: *Talk about the people in your kids' lives who love them.*

You love your kids. Grandma and Grandpa love them. Who else loves your kids? Neighbors? Friends from Scouts or church or a community group? You may be overwhelmed when you stop to think about who really loves your kids. Help your children recognize this love. If you observe a gift, comment or other gesture from one of these people toward your child, underscore it by saying something like, "I can see she really loves you" or "He really cares about you, doesn't he?" Help your children recognize gestures of love from people outside your family and learn to reciprocate.

HOPEFUL HOUR TIP

 During a family time, engage the whole family in making a comprehensive list of everyone who loves them. See how long the list is. Ask kids to tell you how they know each of these people love them. Talk about how love is a hope-creator that can help kids create the lives they want.

Love Strategy 4: *Love your spouse.*

If you are married, let your kids see you loving each other. Let them witness appropriate displays of affection or hear the kind and encouraging comments you make to each other. Even when you have a disagreement, let kids see how love continues to bind you together and help you solve the problem. Of course, not every disagreement is appropriate for kids to know about. But you might differ on which movie to see or which restaurant to patronize or which household chores should be at the top of the list; everyday experiences like these are a great opportunity to let kids see love in action. Model loving problem-solving and self-sacrifice as a life skill that will help kids create the lives they want for themselves.

HOPEFUL HOUR TIP

 Gather an empty glass jar, scrap paper and pencils. Involve the whole family in the task of filling the jar with ideas for how to show love in action to one another in small, everyday ways. As a follow-up, you might challenge family members to take a slip from the jar and express that action at a time that might pleasantly surprise someone else.

LOVE ASSIGNMENTS

LOVE Assignment 1: *Reflect on expressions of love that are meaningful to you.*

Set aside some time to reflect on various stages of your own childhood and adolescence. What specific expressions of love were the most meaningful to you? Plan a time to share these memories with your family. Then have each of your kids do the same following your memory-sharing experience. Set a good example here and your children will be compelled to follow your lead.

LOVE Assignment 2: *Plan a family act of love.*

Give your kids a chance to see the power of love in action by being on the giving end, not just the receiving end. Use one Hopeful Hour to plan a family activity that would demonstrate love to someone outside your family and use a second Hopeful Hour to carry out your plan.

HOPEFUL HOUR PLANNING PAGE

Write in your own words the main substance of Principle 7: LOVE

```
┌─────────────────────────────────────────────┐
│                                               │
│   _____   │
│                                               │
│   _____   │
│                                               │
│   _____   │
│                                               │
└─────────────────────────────────────────────┘
```

Plan how many Hopeful Hours you think you'll need to devote to this principle. List the dates you will have these Hopeful Hours. Jot down a key activity you will use in each Hopeful Hour to engage your children in learning the principle. Your activities may be suggestions you find in the chapter or adaptations you know your child will enjoy. Make sure your plan includes all the key strategies of the principle. Continue on an additional sheet of paper if necessary.

	Date	Strategy	Key Activity

CHAPTER 12

Do You Have a Hopeful Kid?

The moment of truth has arrived. Fast-forward a few months or even a few years. Imagine you've been investing in HOPEFUL all this time. You've diligently applied all the principles and strategies and completed all the assignments. You've watched your child grow in many dimensions. Is your child a Hopeful Kid? You might be wondering and speculating one way or the other. You may have a good idea. Nevertheless, I strongly encourage you to ask. Just ask your child, "Do you believe you can create the life you want through positive choices and goals?"

If you've invested time and energy in HOPEFUL and followed through on the strategies, your child will be familiar with these words. You will have been asking your child to repeat the Hopeful Motto all along. It's a big question, and you'll likely ask it more than once. Younger children can grasp the significance of the question on a basic level, especially with your help in identifying positive and negative choices. Older kids and teens will begin to realize that it's actually a complex question and one that they must learn to ask themselves at critical decision points.

So ask the question. Then listen carefully to the answer.

IF THE ANSWER IS YES

When your kid answers "Yes" to the Hopeful Motto question, congratulations are in order because he or she has learned to be a Hopeful Kid, and your HOPEFUL journey is complete. However, where the journey ends, the way of life begins. Therefore, your job now is to help your kid maintain a hopeful way of life. You will best accomplish this by continuing to reinforce HOPEFUL principles during Hopeful Hours. Yes, you need to stick with your HOPEFUL Hours in order to help your child maintain a hopeful way of life and to prepare your child to live independently.

The only difference now is that your child needs to take a more active role in determining which strategies to work on to maintain a hopeful way of life. To get this process started, ask this question during Hopeful Hours: "Which strategy do you want to work on right now to help you stay hopeful?" Then have your child look over the various strategies that make up the Hopeful Kids Action Plan and choose what best fits his or her needs. (Note: some of the strategies are meant only for parents to complete.) If you feel your child is not ready to independently make this kind of assessment, then you need to determine what to work on to maintain hopeful growth. Just remember to keep asking the Hopeful Motto question and involve kids in the process of setting strategy. Eventually they will be able to determine on their own what they need to work on to continue a hopeful way life.

You also need to constantly pay attention to behavior to determine if kids are making choices that result in hopeful outcomes. Be especially vigilant for hope-suckers that start to drag kids down and cause them to lose hopeful momentum. If this is the case, use Hope Testing to get kids back on a positive path by replacing the hope-suckers with hope-creators. For example, if a child is having difficulty expressing feelings, refer to Principle 2: OPEN and re-teach how to be assertive. If a child seems to be anxious about the future, refer to Principle 3: PURPOSE to reaffirm and re-establish goals. If a child is making poor choices that result in negative outcomes, work on sharpening her problem-solving skills with Principle 5: FIND. If you don't know why a child is acting in a manner incompatible with hopefulness, refer to Principle 6: UNDERSTAND; ask questions, and listen to answers. And if a child gets involved in something beyond your resources to resolve, then find help! Ultimately, you will have to use your hopeful knowledge and skills to determine what needs to be done to keep your child on track when someone or something tries to derail him or her. Remember, nothing—absolutely nothing—is worth your kid's right to live hopefully.

IF THE ANSWER IS NO

If you ask your child, "Do you believe you can create the life you want through positive choices and goals?" and the answer is no, don't panic. All this means is that you and your child have a little more work to do. Some kids will have trouble answering affirmatively because they recognize they don't fully understand all the HOPEFUL principles. Others may hesitate to say yes because they recognize the complexity of the question. Perhaps they don't feel ready to make independent evaluations and decisions. Some open communication will help you discover where the glitch is, and you can work on that.

Hope Testing is a great place to start. This will help you to identify what hope-suckers are sabotaging your kid's efforts to become hopeful. Once you have determined this, you can work to replace these negative issues with positive hope-creators. Show your child the Hopeful Kids Action Plan and ask, "Which strategies do you feel you need to work on in order to believe you can create the life you want?" If you don't think the child can answer this question, ask questions and listen to answers to see what clues you turn up. This will reveal the specific strategies a child needs to relearn in order to get where he or she needs to be. Once again, if you can't help, find the resources that can. The key is to stay committed to the HOPEFUL process until your child says, "I believe I can create the life I want through positive choices and goals." Believe it—get it!

THE HOPEFUL KIDS ACTION PLAN

At the end of the book you'll find the Hopeful Kids Action Plan. This is a summary of the seven key principles and related strategies in a checklist format. Use this tool to keep track of your progress as you complete each strategy. This way you will know when you have completed your entire action plan. Do this until you have completed every strategy listed in the plan, one by one. When you have finished doing this, you will be ready to determine if your child has become a Hopeful Kid. To make this easy for you, a check-off box is provided for every strategy. Your child must experience everything HOPEFUL has to offer before he or she is ready to be a Hopeful Kid. And finally, remember to personalize your plan by writing your family's name in the title line.

You are almost there. Prepare to empower your kids by taking action—hopeful action.

The Hopeful Kids Action Plan

for the _____ *Family.*

Mission: My mission is to develop my children into Hopeful Kids.
I will successfully accomplish this mission by completing each strategy
of HOPEFUL KIDS.

PRINCIPLE 1: HOUR
Objective 1: Invest one hour of hope in your child per month.

□ HOUR Strategy 1. Create a Hopeful Hour for your children.

□ HOUR Strategy 2. Create value for your Hopeful Hour.

□ HOUR Strategy 3. Dedicate all of your Hopeful Hours to completing all of the strategies of HOPEFUL.

PRINCIPLE 2: OPEN
Objective 2: Be open with your child.

□ OPEN Strategy 1. Be the first to influence your children by making them your first priority.

□ OPEN Strategy 2. Be willing to talk with your son or daughter about anything, anytime, anywhere—no limits!

□ OPEN Strategy 3. Risk first. Take the first step to being open by admitting your fears.

□ OPEN Strategy 4. Be more open by paying attention to your body language and voice tone.

☐ OPEN Strategy 5. Teach openness by practicing the three R's: Receive, Respect, Respond.

☐ OPEN Strategy 6. Take Ten and Think–Choose–Act. Teach and practice these strategies whenever you or your child feels upset.

☐ OPEN Strategy 7. Ask this question when you or your child feels angry: "Do I feel in control?"

☐ OPEN Strategy 8. Teach your children how to openly express their feelings by being assertive.

PRINCIPLE 3: PURPOSE
Objective 3a: Discovering your child's purpose.

☐ PURPOSE Strategy 1. Teach your child the Hopeful Motto: "I can create the life I want through positive choices and goals."

☐ PURPOSE Strategy 2. Remind yourself on a daily basis that your primary purpose is to help your child become a Hopeful Kid.

☐ PURPOSE Strategy 3. Use the P-5 Method to discover your child's PURPOSE: 1. Positive 2. Passion 3. Purpose 4. Plan 5.Power

Objective 3b: Reinforcing your child's purpose.

☐ PURPOSE Strategy 4. Teach your child the power of choice.

☐ PURPOSE Strategy 5. Create many mini-opportunities for success.

☐ PURPOSE Strategy 6. Schedule purposeful experiences.

☐ PURPOSE Strategy 7. Reinforce the positive: Believe it—get it!

☐ PURPOSE Strategy 8. Reward the behavior you want.

☐ PURPOSE Strategy 9. No failure; only feedback.

☐ PURPOSE Strategy 10. Strengthen your child's ability to make purposeful and responsible choices through independent evaluation.

☐ PURPOSE Strategy 11. BULL'S-EYE—a unique approach for keeping your child on target with purpose.

☐ PURPOSE Strategy 12. Conduct periodic tune-ups.

PRINCIPLE 4: EXAMPLE
Objective 4: Be a hopeful example for your child.

☐ EXAMPLE Strategy 1. Be an effective Hopeful Example by learning and applying The Hopeful Example Ten Commandments.

☐ EXAMPLE Strategy 2. Awareness: Be a more conscious and influential Hopeful Example by identifying your hope-encouraging and hope-discouraging behaviors.

☐ EXAMPLE Strategy 3. Action Plan: Strengthen and increase the frequency of your hope-encouraging behaviors by developing a Hopeful Example Action Plan.

☐ EXAMPLE Strategy 4. Habit Formation: Be an effective Hopeful Example for your children by converting your hope-encouraging behaviors into a hopeful habit.

PRINCIPLE 5: FIND
Objective 5: Teach your child how to find solutions.

☐ FIND Strategy 1. Learn the D-BEST method to systematically problem-solve and find solutions.

☐ FIND Strategy 2. Teach the D-BEST method during Hopeful Hour

☐ FIND Strategy 3. Encourage a habit of using D-BEST.

PRINCIPLE 6: UNDERSTAND
Objective 6a: Learn to ask questions and listen to your child.

☐ UNDERSTAND Strategy 1. Show your child that you care by asking questions based on the five Ws and How: Who, What, When, Where, Why, and How?

☐ UNDERSTAND Strategy 2. Listen to your child and you will understand.

☐ UNDERSTAND Strategy 3. Ask your child a positive question every day.

☐ UNDERSTAND Strategy 4. Learn to better understand your child by playing The Asking-and-Listening Game.

Objective 6b: Teach your child to recognize hope-suckers and hope-creators.

☐ UNDERSTAND Strategy 5. Identify your child's hope-creators and hope-suckers.
☐ UNDERSTAND Strategy 6. Teach the Hope Testing technique.
☐ UNDERSTAND Strategy 7. Replace negative self-talk with hopeful talk.

PRINCIPLE 7: LOVE
Objective 7: Demonstrate love to your children in specific actions.

☐ LOVE Strategy 1. Tell your child, "I love you" every single day.
☐ LOVE Strategy 2. Show love in actions.
☐ LOVE Strategy 3. Talk about the people in your kids' lives who love them.
☐ LOVE Strategy 4. Love your spouse.

RECRUITING HOPE STARS

Hey, does your family want to be in one of my upcoming videos for Hopeful Kids? Or, would you like to appear as a hope star on my website and future Hopeful Kids' products?

Great. Let me tell you how. Go to my website: **www.hopefulkids. com**, then, click on the "My Hope Star Story" link and share your experience about how this book helped you develop Hopeful Kids and become a hopeful family. Also, you can check in periodically and share your hopeful journey successes and insights. We will select those stories that best communicate the hopeful-kids' experience and how it helped you unleash your sons' and daughters' personal power. These stories will be used for future videos or projects and to give hope to other families. I look forward to hearing from you soon. Until then, take action, fulfill your mission and become a hopeful family.

Website: **www.hopefulkids.com**

ENDORSEMENTS

"All parents hope their children will 'turn out'. Yet, with great consequence, many parents lack the knowledge and skills necessary to accomplish this. As a family counselor, husband and parent of 6 children I am grateful to Dr. Cash for writing Hopeful Kids. Reading each inspiring chapter, I realized that only a person with Dr. Cash's experience, insights and success could create such a comprehensive work. Proven strategies and step-by-step exercises will equip you and your kids to engage a life full of hope."

> *Keith Dorscht, MTS*
> *Founder and President, Live Fully Engaged Ministries*

"Leonard Cash has developed a wonderful prescription for helping our children see and experience the hope in life – something we all would like for our children. His thoughtful and detailed program helps parents focus on the positives and break down the huge tasks of parenting into understandable and doable activities. This is an excellent resource and reference that parents can return to again and again."

> *Bob Cooper, MSW President*
> *CEO Tennyson Center for Children*

"Hopeful kids is useful when teachers are talking with parents and providing them with strategies for how to support their children as they grow through the K-12 years. This would be particularly true in the elementary years (and possibly in middle school years) -- as this is the time when teachers and parents have the most contact."

> *Lisa R. Horwitch, Ph.D.*
> *K-12 Teacher and Education Policy & Reform Consultant*

"I found this book to do a very thorough job of focusing on a topic few have identified as important in the lives of youth at risk. These youth come from families, neighborhoods, and schools where hope is in short supply. Dr. Cash identifies the critical role of hope for improving people's adjustment and happiness. The book is especially timely given the economy and substantially greater stress on families.

Hopeful Kids is a very useful book for parents who want to implement a philosophy and practices that foster hope. It is so timely and gives parents great tools for empowering themselves and their kids that do not cost money. Dr. Cash has taken an underused concept and applied it in clear detail so that parents can improve the quality of their family life."

Don Gordon, Ph.D.
Professor of Psychology Emeritus, Ohio University
CEO, Family Works Inc.

"Leonard Cash - "Dr. Hope" - has developed a simple yet straightforward set of seven working principles for kids and their parents that can guide them to more successful and constructive lives. His elegant model demonstrates through multiple examples how kids can be empowered when they have hope: hope for their futures; hope that leads to personal growth; hope on how to relate to others; and hope on how to become a victor instead of a victim. This very readable book undoubtedly will prove helpful as well for juvenile justice practitioners who work with troubled kids on a day-to-day basis."

Dr. Alvin W. Cohn, Criminologist
President of Administration of Justice Services, Inc.

"Dr. Cash goes through important steps to improving openness, assertiveness, communication, and the fostering of hope with great tools in a doable, relatable way."

Stephanie Pauline
More than Music Inc.